**books**online

Read this book online today:

With SAP PRESS BooksOnline we offer you online access to knowledge from the leading SAP experts. Whether you use it as a beneficial supplement or as an alternative to the printed book, with SAP PRESS BooksOnline you can:

- Access your book anywhere, at any time. All you need is an Internet connection.
- Perform full text searches on your book and on the entire SAP PRESS library.
- Build your own personalized SAP library.

The SAP PRESS customer advantage:

Register this book today at *www.sap-press.com* and obtain exclusive free trial access to its online version. If you like it (and we think you will), you can choose to purchase permanent, unrestricted access to the online edition at a very special price!

Here's how to get started:

1. Visit *www.sap-press.com*.
2. Click on the link for SAP PRESS BooksOnline and login (or create an account).
3. Enter your free trial license key, shown below in the corner of the page.
4. Try out your online book with full, unrestricted access for a limited time!

Your personal free trial **license key**
for this online book is:

pfu6-gcbd-msi8-7vnw

Implementing SAP® Enhancement Packages

PRESS

SAP® Essentials

Expert SAP knowledge for your day-to-day work

Whether you wish to expand your SAP knowledge, deepen it, or master a use case, SAP Essentials provide you with targeted expert knowledge that helps support you in your day-to-day work. To the point, detailed, and ready to use.

SAP PRESS is a joint initiative of SAP and Galileo Press. The know-how offered by SAP specialists combined with the expertise of the Galileo Press publishing house offers the reader expert books in the field. SAP PRESS features first-hand information and expert advice, and provides useful skills for professional decision-making.

SAP PRESS offers a variety of books on technical and business related topics for the SAP user. For further information, please visit our website: *www.sap-press.com.*

Marc O. Schäfer, Matthias Melich
SAP Solution Manager Enterprise Edition
2009, app. 550 pp.
978-1-59229-271-4

Gerhard Oswald, Uwe Hommel
SAP Enterprise Support
2009, app. 350 pp
978-1-59229-302-5

Alan Rickayzen, Jocelyn Dart, Ginger Gatling
Practical Workflow for SAP
2009, app. 1,000 pp.
978-1-59229-285-1

Markus Helfen, Michael Lauer, Hans Martin Trauthwein
Testing SAP Solutions
2007, app. 350 pp.
978-1-59229-127-4

Martina Kaplan and Christian Oehler

Implementing SAP® Enhancement Packages

Galileo Press

Bonn • Boston

Galileo Press is named after the Italian physicist, mathematician and philosopher Galileo Galilei (1564–1642). He is known as one of the founders of modern science and an advocate of our contemporary, heliocentric worldview. His words *Eppur se muove* (And yet it moves) have become legendary. The Galileo Press logo depicts Jupiter orbited by the four Galilean moons, which were discovered by Galileo in 1610.

Editor Maike Lübbers
English Edition Editor Kelly Grace Harris
Translation Lemoine International, Inc., Salt Lake City, UT
Copyeditor Michael Beady
Cover Design Graham Geary
Photo Credit Fotolia/Marco Becker
Layout Design Vera Brauner
Production Editor Kelly O'Callaghan
Assistant Production Editor Graham Geary
Typesetting Publishers' Design and Production Services, Inc.
Printed and bound in Canada

ISBN 978-1-59229-351-3

1st Edition 2011

1st German edition published 2010 by Galileo Press, Bonn, Germany

Library of Congress Cataloging-in-Publication Data
Kaplan, Martina.
Implementing SAP Enhancement Packages / Martina Kaplan, Christian Oehler.—1st ed.
   p. cm.
Includes bibliographical references and index.
ISBN-13: 978-1-59229-351-3 (alk. paper)
ISBN-10: 1-59229-351-4 (alk. paper)
1. Integrated software. 2. Business--Data processing. I. Oehler, Christian. II. Title.
QA76.76.I57K37 2010
005.5—dc22

2010015317

Contents

Foreword

Nothing is as persistent as the constant change of the markets. Thanks to globalization and ever-increasing networking, the effects of sudden changes outside of enterprises continuously grow, and the reasons for these changes become more complex and more difficult to predict. Successful enterprises must find answers to these challenges to remain competitive for the long term. In this context, flexibility is a major factor for success, because if enterprises can swiftly respond to external changes, they can keep themselves profitable. Standard SAP software is an integral part in answering these challenges, because it enables enterprises to respond to new business challenges in a strategic and operationally suitable way.

Up to now, however, it has been a major challenge for customers to quickly and easily install new functionality to have a state-of-the-art system; often, upgrade projects had to be implemented to use the most current functions of a new release. Because an upgrade also entails updating numerous functions and user interfaces, this often results in high adaption, tests, and additional training for the customer's project, which, in turn, leads to postponements of upgrade projects and innovation gaps for the customer.

With enhancement packages, which were initially provided for SAP ERP and are now planned to be the delivery model for the entire SAP Business Suite in the future, SAP has found a way to bridge this innovation gap. Enhancement packages let customers implement the required functions selectively and with little effort. The core of the new delivery strategy lies in an improved software lifecycle: With enhancement packages, customers can install new functionality in a targeted manner and activate them in a decoupled approach. In this process, SAP enhancement packages are imported into the system as part of regular maintenance work in combination with support packages, invisible for the end-user. The customer can then activate and implement the functions required. This way, the technical update and operational use of the new functionality are decoupled from one another.

This also ensures a higher stability of the processes from an end-user's perspective, because new functions are only activated in the requested locations using the new Switch Framework. In all other areas, the end user won't notice any difference in the existing user interfaces and standard SAP processes. Thus, SAP offers its customers a practical way to utilize SAP's most current software innovations at regular intervals. The result is a high number of enhancement package customers; currently, more than 6,500 customers have already used this method. Due to this success, SAP plans to expand the enhancement package concept to the entire SAP Business Suite over the next few years, including SAP Customer Relationship Management (CRM), SAP Supply Chain Management (SCM), SAP Supplier Relationship Management (SRM), and SAP Product Lifecycle Management (PLM).

The two authors, Martina Kaplan and Christian Oehler, are enhancement package experts who know everything from concept to practical implementation. In this book, they incorporate experience that they've gained in supporting and consulting many customers from different market segments. They are supported by coauthors Torsten Kamenz, Andreas Kemmler, and Frank Zweissig, who imparted their expertise from an architecture and development perspective. Thus, this book provides the readers with valuable information on both architectural and technical backgrounds — essential for developers, administrators, and architects; and on the practical implementation, which is critical for project leads, technical experts, and administrators.

We hope that this book will help readers gain profound insights in the enhancement package concept and its efficient use in real-life projects.

Joachim Hechler, Head of SAP Business Suite Development
Klemens Gramlich, Senior Vice President ERP Development

Preface

In this book, it is our pleasure to present to you information about the functionality and implementation of SAP enhancement packages. Since the delivery of the first enhancement packages in 2007, we've supported SAP's latest delivery strategy. In numerous presentations, workshops, and customer projects, we have described and implemented the enhancement package concept for customers in the United States, Australia, China, India, and in Europe. Thanks to a high level of interest from these customers, and a vast number of customer requests, we decided to write this book. This is the first book on enhancement packages available on the market. It is the culmination of our experience with enhancement packages presented in a comprehensive manner.

The demand for SAP's latest delivery strategy is huge: In just three years, more than 6,500 customers have used enhancement packages in live operation. Initially, it all started with SAP ERP; currently, it functions as the standard delivery concept for the entire SAP Business Suite.

The current enhancement package has been available since May 5, 2009, and is called *enhancement package 4 for SAP ERP*, which is what our book refers to. The book is structured as follows:

Chapter 1, Introduction, presents an introduction and overview of enhancement packages.

Chapter 2, Architecture and Technology, focuses on the architectural and developmental aspects of enhancement packages, especially the use of the Switch Framework. We'll first discuss the reintegration of industry solutions in SAP ERP, because this formed the basis for the development of SAP enhancement packages, and then we'll describe the architecture of SAP enhancement packages in general and the properties of enhancement package 4 for SAP ERP in particular.

Chapter 3, Successful EHP Project Management, discusses the project-planning aspects of enhancement packages. The chapter starts with an overview of the five success factors of enhancement projects, which is followed by a description of all relevant phases and activities. A real-life example and useful tips are also included.

Chapter 4, Implementation Tools and Service Offers, outlines the role of SAP Solution Manager in the installation process. In a step-by-step description, you'll learn which settings are required, and how to download enhancement packages using a maintenance transaction. Then we'll look at a new installation tool — SAP EHP Installer. In addition to the structure of the tool, we'll also discuss its technical procedures and a detailed description of the installation process phases. There is also an overview of the additional utilities and support services offers for installing enhancement packages.

Chapter 5, Practical Experiences and Tips on Enhancement Package Installations, provides some real-life experiences to support you in the technical implementation of your enhancement package. Some background information on the analysis and optimization of enhancement package installations is also included.

This book is primarily aimed at customers and partners in an SAP environment with an interest in SAP technology; for example, technical consultants, administrators, developers, and project leads. But it is also useful for anyone with an interest in enhancement packages.

Acknowledgments

Books can never be produced without the support and collaboration of many individuals. Therefore, we would like to take this opportunity to thank all our SAP colleagues who helped with the creation of this book, particularly for the many conversations, tips, and valuable discussions: Alexander Achterfeld, Jens Baumann, Stefan Berndt, Matthias Brühl, Martina David, Stefan Discher, Stefan Elfner, Tilman Goettke, Ingo Heinke, Ralf Kau, Armin Koesegi, Oliver Kroneisen, Jürgen Mair, Anja Müller, Robert Pinzke, Stefan Raffel, Heike Ripp, Marc Oliver Schäfer, Benjamin Schneider, Jörg Schön, Suzanne Ullmann, and Marcus Wefers.

This chapter introduces you to SAP enhancement packages. You'll learn about the ideas behind this enhancement strategy and its benefits.

1 Introduction

With enhancement packages for SAP ERP, SAP has created a new delivery concept that enables customers to flexibly implement new functions with minimal effort. SAP enhancement packages include new, optional functions for existing SAP applications, such as cross-industry and industry-specific functions, simplified user interfaces, and enterprise services. Therefore, enhancement packages are the cornerstones of SAP's latest delivery strategy, and replace the previous strategy of standard releases. For many customers, the new enhancement packages supersede the previously required and often elaborate upgrade projects.

In the past, SAP customers implemented a release change about every four to six years. Here, maintenance was the main criterion rather than the business and technical innovations. The reason for four to six years between release changes was that the release change often entailed unnecessary functional changes to the application which, in turn, required a lot of adaption work, tests, and customer training.

At the same time, users had a need for business process improvements that were available in the latest releases. However, the improvements for individual users were not enough when compared to the upcoming implementation and upgrade change for all users. The *Chief Information Officer* (CIO) of an enterprise usually handles any conflict between innovation requirements and demand for continuity; on the one hand, he must safeguard critical SAP systems required for running business activities. On the other hand, he must provide new functions to the business user to improve the business processes and keep the enterprise's competitive edge. With SAP enhancement packages, SAP has created an enhancement concept that enables simplified access to new functions, avoiding the extensive effects of an upgrade, and therefore resolving the conflict between innovation and stability

(Figure 1.1). With enhancement packages, customers can import new functions in a targeted manner and activate them without a technical installation.

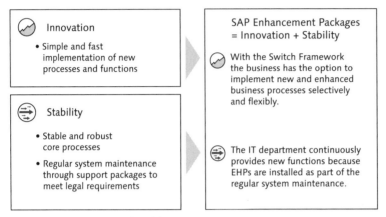

Figure 1.1 Innovation and Stability

When you use SAP enhancement packages, the new functions are imported with support packages during regular maintenance work; however, they are not activated and implemented until they are required. Customer systems operating with a release that doesn't yet support enhancement packages (for example, releases prior to SAP ERP 6.0) can integrate the respective current enhancement package within the scope of the upgrade project.

Because functions that are newly installed from enhancement packages must be activated via the Switch Framework, users won't notice any difference in the user interfaces or in the SAP transactions or processes after the enhancement package is installed.

The selective activation of new functions and user interfaces contributes to filling the "innovation gap" (see Figure 1.2). So new "business functions" can be provided to the user department *on demand* (instead of every four to six years).

Customers can use enhancement packages to ensure that their business processes always meet the most current requirements of their business areas. By separating the technical installation as part of the maintenance from activating business functions, business areas can individually implement and use the required function, independent of the time of installation.

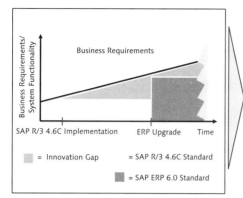
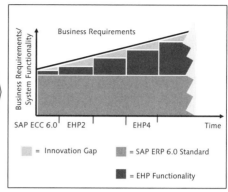

Figure 1.2 Improved Software Lifecycle

> **Note**
>
> A business function (BF) is self-contained. From a technical point of view, business functions consist of individual switches that can be used to activate code, menu entries, and customizing activities in the Implementation Guide (IMG). When you switch on a BF, this activates all of the technical switches that belong to this BF. After you've activated a business function, the following changes and developments become visible:
>
> ► Menu entries
>
> ► New fields in the user interfaces
>
> ► New activities in the IMG
>
> Chapter 2, Section 2.2, Architecture of Enhancement Packages, provides more information on this topic.

SAP ERP 6.0 was the first SAP application for which SAP launched enhancement packages. Enhancement package 4 for SAP ERP 6.0 has been part of the standard delivery since May 5, 2009. For this reason, this book focuses on this enhancement package, whose functionally also includes the enhancements of enhancement packages 1 through 3. Chapter 2, Section 2.3, Development of Enhancement Packages, provides additional details. Functions and further developments within the framework of the product strategy are also provided continuously via enhancement packages for other core SAP Business Suite applications. You can find more information in the document, "SAP's Release Strategy for Large Enterprises," which is available on the SAP Service Marketplace (*http://service.sap.com/releasestrategy*).

Core SAP Business Suite Applications

Core SAP Business Suite applications include the following:

▶ SAP ERP

▶ SAP Customer Relationship Management (CRM)

▶ SAP Supply Chain Management (SCM)

▶ SAP Supplier Relationship Management (SRM)

▶ SAP Product Lifecycle Management (PLM)

In addition, special *industry applications* and *supplementary applications* are part of SAP Business Suite. As mentioned previously, you can find a complete overview at *http://service.sap.com/releasestrategy*.

Therefore, most parts of the enhancement package concept, which is based on SAP ERP, are also valid for other core applications of SAP Business Suite and most of the industry solutions based on this concept.

1.1 SAP Enhancement Packages — from the Idea to the Implementation

The enhancement package concept is based on the fact that most customers maintain their systems at regular intervals to keep them current and meet any relevant legal requirements. To do this, customers usually import *Support Packages* (SPs) to their SAP system annually.

Note

The following terms are used synonymously in this book:

▶ *Install* and *import*

▶ *Switch on* and *activate*

The combination of installation and activation is referred to as *enhancement package implementation*.

Most information technology (IT) organizations have a clearly structured and defined IT schedule, including maintenance cycles. For SAP customers, it is of great significance that support packages only contain corrections and updates due to legal changes. This prevents end users from suddenly having to use new functions and process flows even though it is not required operationally. Because most customers import support packages regularly, it was an obvious decision to provide new, optional business functions and user interfaces bound with the support packages — as long as their installation remains "invisible" to the end users and they can be activated as needed.

A new technology, *Switch Framework*, was delivered as part of SAP NetWeaver 7.0 within the SAP NetWeaver Application Server (AS) ABAP. Using the Switch Framework, it was, for the first time, possible to control the "visibility" of new functions via technical *switches*. In this context, the Switch Framework acts as a control center. When you activate selected business functions, you trigger system changes — for example, the generation of new object versions — to "release" the new functions. The new technology was used for the first time within the reintegration of SAP industry solutions with SAP ERP, and was therefore available in *SAP ERP Central Component* (ECC) together with SAP ERP 6.0. (See Chapter 2, Section 2.1, Brief Introduction to the Development of the SAP ERP Architecture, for more detailed information about this.) So the Switch Framework passed its test and was available for other usage scenarios.

As a result, SAP was able to meet its customers' continuously growing demand for a simplified way to provide new functions, and the idea of SAP enhancement packages was born. SAP provides optional enhancement packages as part of the regular system maintenance with support packages; they don't cause any changes to the existing user interfaces and processes for the end user during the technical installation. To utilize these new functions, you must activate them in a second step (see Figure 1.3).

Enhancement packages consist of selectively installable and activatable units. This minimizes installation, on the one hand, and ensures the targeted implementation of new functionality as required, on the other hand. The following sections describe the two basic principles in more detail.

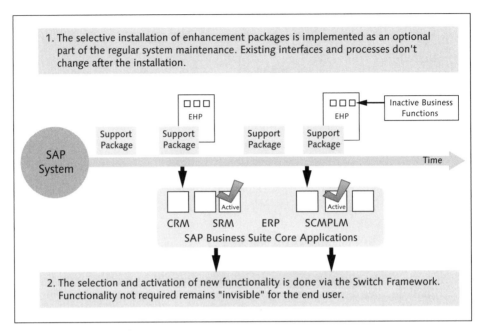

Figure 1.3 Basic Principles

1.1.1 Selective Installation

A new option is to use SAP enhancement packages to only update parts of SAP ERP 6.0 (particularly on the SAP ECC Server), depending on the functions selected by the customer. In earlier releases, you always had to update all parts of an application.

> **Example**
>
> The customer wants to utilize the latest SAP ERP Human Capital Management functions, for example, *Employee Interaction Center*, which the human resources (HR) department can use to improve efficiency and employee satisfaction in HR processes. The HCM_EIC_CI_2 business function is implemented via the technical usage, Human Capital Management. During the next maintenance process, the customer must select this technical usage in SAP Solution Manager for the system to automatically download the corresponding packages, in addition to the latest support packages, and install them in a second step.

Chapter 2, Section 2.2, discusses the architecture and the terms *business function* and *technical usage* in greater detail.

1.1.2 Selective Activation

Another innovation with regard to the simplification of the implementation process includes business functions, with which you can encapsulate new functions in an economically reasonable way. With enhancement package 4, there are approximately 300 activatable business functions available.

Figure 1.4 illustrates how customers can select and install technical usages in the first step (❶). This updates specific software components. In the second step (❷), specific business functions are activated, and the new functions become "visible" in the system.

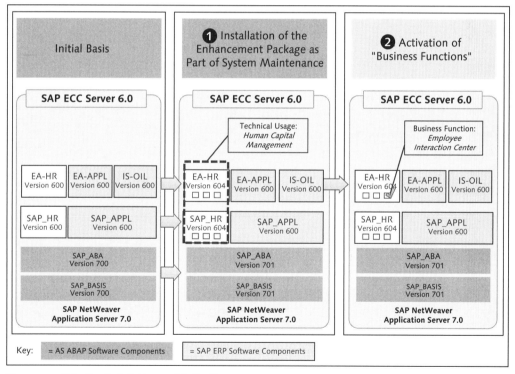

Figure 1.4 Selective Installation and Activation

From a technical perspective, every enhancement package consists of new versions of existing software components; for example, software component SAP_APPL 604. They are grouped in technical usages and delivered. Then customers can download appropriate selections from SAP Solution Manager and install them later on. Chapter 2, Architecture and Technology, provides further information on the architecture and business functions.

Conclusion

The Enhancement Package concept with its selective installation and decoupled activation helps to fill the innovation gap in many enterprises. The new delivery strategy further optimizes the software lifecycle: Customers can now implement and use new functions easier and with less effort.

"He who wants to build high towers must dwell with the foundation for a long time." (Anton Bruckner)

This chapter lays the foundation for subsequent chapters by describing the basic architecture and development of SAP enhancement packages.

2 Architecture and Technology

This chapter provides an overview of the development of the SAP ERP application architecture. It contains a detailed description of the Switch Framework within the scope of integrating industry solutions with SAP ERP, and then explains the development guidelines and architecture of SAP enhancement packages.

2.1 Brief Introduction to the Development of the SAP ERP Architecture

SAP ERP's success story starts with the introduction of the first mainframe-based solution, SAP R/2. In the early 1990s, SAP R/3 was the first integrated business solution that was based on a client-server architecture. At that time, SAP mainly used ABAP to develop the SAP ERP solution. With SAP R/3 4.7 (SAP R/3 Enterprise), Unicode was supported for the first time.

Figure 2.1 shows how the SAP ERP solution has developed from a monolithic SAP R/3 to a distributed application with SAP ERP 6.0. The primary difference between SAP ERP and SAP R/3 is that SAP ERP is based on SAP NetWeaver, which is SAP's integrated technology platform that forms the foundation for all applications of SAP Business Suite. Among other things, SAP NetWeaver is comprised of the components for process integration (SAP NetWeaver Process Integration (PI)), information integration (SAP NetWeaver Business Warehouse (BW)), and user integration (SAP NetWeaver Portal).

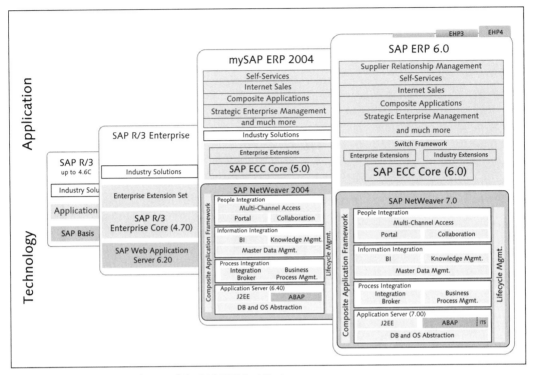

Figure 2.1 Evolution of the SAP ERP Architecture

With SAP ERP, new functions were delivered not as part of the previous SAP R/3, but as self-contained components or systems. This way, the integral parts can be implemented in ABAP and Java. Some SAP NetWeaver components are based on Java (for example, SAP NetWeaver Portal) or on ABAP and Java (for example, SAP NetWeaver PI). The main component of SAP ERP is called SAP ERP Central Component (ECC); it is the technical successor of SAP R/3 and is based on ABAP.

With SAP ERP 6.0, most of the industry solutions were returned to the standard for the first time. Technically, this laid the foundation for the subsequent development of SAP enhancement packages. Next, we'll look at an overview of the development of SAP industry solutions.

2.1.1 SAP Industry Solutions

Let's go back to the late 1990s. After SAP had developed the basic processes for Financial Accounting (FI), Controlling (CO), human resources (HR), and logistics in SAP R/2 and SAP R/3 (in the 1980s and 1990s) and launched them with great success, many enterprises asked for industry-specific solutions that were supposed to be based on the existing standard business software. They wanted enterprise software that met the special requirements of their industry to avoid elaborate custom developments.

This was the starting point for developing industry solutions at SAP. The industry solutions were implemented either as an integral part of the product, such as SAP R/3 (enhancement of the standard version), or as an add-on software product based on SAP R/3. If the business and functional requirements were relevant for several industries, the standard version was enhanced; an example of this is integrated batch management, a requirement coming from the chemicals industry. Because batch management is also relevant to other industries, it was integrated with the SAP R/3 system at an early stage.

If the business requirement was only relevant for one or a few industries, however, an industry-specific add-on was used instead; an example of this is the solution for the oil and gas industry (IS-Oil). This add-on is based on SAP R/3 and enhances already-existing processes and scenarios. Due to the many requirements of various customers and customer groups from different industries, SAP developed multiple industry-specific add-ons. Frequently, customers were organized in special interest groups that represented the respective industry toward SAP — an example would be the Oil & Gas Global Industry Advisory Council (GIAC), where ten oil companies agree on development requirements, their prioritization, and the desired delivery schedules of the entire industry. Here, SAP industry development collaborated specifically and directly with the customers, allowing well-coordinated functions to be launched quickly.

However, there were also some disadvantages from the customer's perspective: Some add-ons were delivered with a time delay for the underlying basis release. For example, the IS-Oil version for SAP R/3 4.6C was launched approximately one year after the standard delivery of SAP R/3 4.6C. Consequently, the latest SAP functions could not be used right away. The support packages (SPs) were also not available until later, whereas the period between the SPs for standard systems and those for add-on systems was considerably shorter. As a result of the delayed delivery, many customers had to build an additional standard system to use SPs to import corrections and important updates of the software due to legal changes.

The more than 20 industry solutions developed by SAP were very successful. For example, the world's ten largest oil companies use SAP IS-Oil; overall, several hundred customers use this solution in production.

2.1.2 Integration of Industry Solutions with the Standard SAP ERP Solution

After most industry solutions had reached a certain level of functionality, customers more and more frequently concerned themselves with the technical disadvantages of the industry add-ons. Thus, SAP started to focus on making industry solutions an integral part of SAP ECC again. Among other things, this would enable customers to receive corrections and important updates promptly, and help to consolidate their system landscapes.

A basic prerequisite for this process is a framework that is integrated with the existing development environment and enables the "switching" of functions, ensuring that customers can only utilize the functions they need. This resulted in the *Switch Framework* concept. You can use the Switch Framework to control the visibility of repository objects or their components via switches.

The existing software component model was also enhanced by industry extensions (for example, IS-Oil), which comprised a large part of industry-specific developments. Within the Switch Framework, industry extensions are represented by *business function sets* (see Figure 2.2). If a customer selects an industry extension — that is, a business function set — he can activate one or more business functions of this industry. Once a business function set is selected and one or more business functions of this set are activated, the customer cannot use *any* other business function sets in the same system.

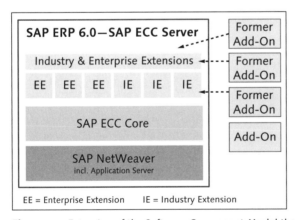

Figure 2.2 Extension of the Software Component Model through Enterprise Extensions

For the integration of industry solutions, some functions of previous industry add-ons were transferred to *enterprise extensions* (see Figure 2.3). As a result, the previously industry-specific functions could be used by all customers without any restrictions. An example is the returnable packaging processing of pallets, which was originally developed for the automotive industry; as of SAP ERP 6.0, it can now be used by customers from any industry (and in combination with other industry solutions). Independent of activating industry business functions, customers can still switch on various generic business functions (enterprise extensions).

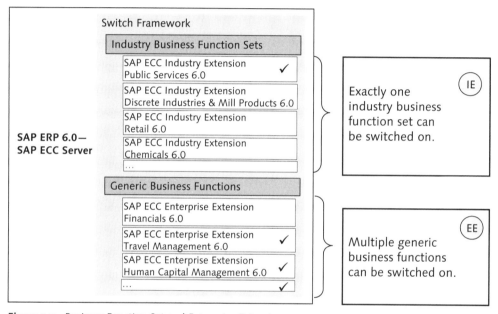

Figure 2.3 Business Function Set and Enterprise Extensions

With SAP ERP 6.0, a lot of SAP industry solutions could be transferred to the standard version via the Switch Framework. This paved the way for further usage scenarios, which we'll look at in the next section.

2.2   Architecture of Enhancement Packages

This section describes the architecture of SAP enhancement packages in general, and the properties of enhancement package 4 for SAP ERP in particular. The use of the Switch Framework to integrate industry solutions with SAP ERP 6.0 formed the basis for the development of SAP enhancement packages.

Definition

Functionally, *SAP enhancement packages for SAP ERP* represent a combination of new and improved business functions. After installation, the customer only needs to activate the new business functions that he actually wants to use.

From a technical point of view, an enhancement package is a combination of specific versions of software components that are part of a defined SAP product version (for example, SAP ERP 6.0), they are delivered together, and can be installed optionally. For the implementation of enhancement packages, you can select which parts are actually supposed to be installed. The smallest installable enhancement package units are the software components that are bundled in a technical usage.

Thanks to selective installation, you can reduce the modification adjustment after installing enhancement packages (for more information on the modification adjustment, refer to Section 2.4.3, Transport of Switch Statuses in System Landscapes). To keep the adjustments for the installed software components as low as possible, the software component versions contained in enhancement packages are delivered as a delta of the previous version. Therefore, only the objects that were actually changed in an enhancement package are delivered in each enhancement package.

All enhancement packages for SAP ERP require the use of Release 6.0. Therefore, SAP ERP 6.0 is also referred to as the basis release for enhancement packages. Installing enhancement packages is optional. SAP ERP 6.0 can also be used without an enhancement package.

After installation, SAP ensures that the new versions of the SAP ERP software components are maintained separately in the enhancement packages and are kept up to date via SAP notes and support packages. This means that besides support packages for SAP ERP 6.0 there are also special support packages for each enhancement package or for each software component version contained in an enhancement package. Here, the support packages for SAP ERP 6.0 and for enhancement packages are synchronized. Corrections of standard functions are contained in support packages for SAP ERP 6.0 and in support packages for enhancement packages. Section 2.2.6, Support Package Strategy and Equivalence Levels, provides more details and a graphical overview of the interaction between the various product versions and support packages.

Initially, no functional changes can be found in the system after parts of an enhancement package have been installed; user interfaces and existing business process can still be used as they were used before (in other words, all existing functionality works correctly). New and changed business functions of an enhancement package must be activated explicitly. By means of the Switch Framework and the Enhancement Framework, SAP ensures that all functional changes can be activated (see Section 2.3, Development of Enhancement Packages).

Enhancement packages are functionally cumulative; that is, an enhancement package is based either on the previous enhancement package or it contains its predecessor (if available). Section 2.2.4, Cumulative Delivery, provides more details on the cumulative behavior of SAP enhancement packages for ERP.

2.2.1 Technical Usages and Product Instances

By means of enhancement packages for SAP ERP 6.0, the smaller, installable units are subdivided into technical usages. Each business function that is delivered in an enhancement package is therefore assigned to a technical usage. It must be installed to activate the corresponding business function. Several business functions can be assigned to a technical usage.

> **Definition**
>
> From a functional perspective, *technical usages* combine software components and the contents of SAP enhancement packages that must be installed jointly, so that a specific business function can be activated. From a technical perspective, a technical usage is a logical grouping unit that comprises interdependent product instances.
>
> Technical usages can only be installed on *existing* product instances. Some examples include Central Applications, Human Capital Management (HCM), and Financial Services (FS).

In the simplest case, a technical usage contains exactly one product instance; for example, a product instance that provides ABAP functions. The technical usage *Human Capital Management*, which provides the business functions for enhancing the HR department for the SAP ECC Server, contains a product instance which, in turn, contains the corresponding ABAP software components; including, SAP_HR 604 and EA-HR 604 (see Figure 2.4).

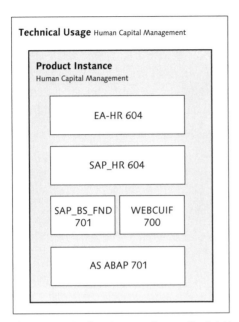

Figure 2.4 Product Instance Human Capital Management

To commission a business function from human resources that refers to the technical usage SAP *Human Capital Management* you must install the software component versions that are summarized in the corresponding product instance Human Capital Management, the SAP ECC Server.

Some technical usages contain multiple instances, because Java applications or portal contents for the business function are provided in addition to the ABAP functions, for example. Figure 2.5 shows the technical usage of *HCM Services*, which also provides the corresponding integration contents (service definitions, integration scenarios, and so on) for SAP NetWeaver PI, in addition to the ABAP functions. Besides the ABAP product instance *Human Capital Management*, it also contains an SAP NetWeaver PI content instance.

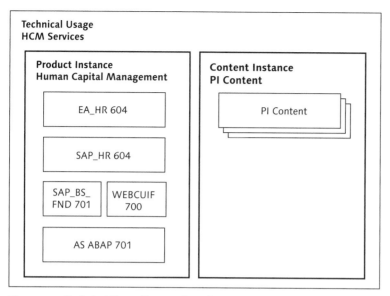

Figure 2.5 Technical Usage Human Capital Management Services

2.2.2   Software Components of Enhancement Package 4 for SAP ERP

A highly integrated software product like SAP ERP comprises numerous relationships between individual software components. You must consider these relationships in the modeling of enhancement packages. Thanks to the option for updating software components selectively by choosing a technical usage, a system can be comprised of system components of different versions after the installation.

For example, EA_HR could be available in version 604 after installation, while SAP_APPL still remains in version 600. The interaction between these different versions regarding cross-component relationships only works if no critical couplings exist between the corresponding enhancement package versions of the software components. A coupling of specific versions of software components is considered critical if a software component completely depends on another one. Therefore, they can only be installed and operated together. Critical couplings are therefore already prevented in the SAP development process of an enhancement package; only uncritical couplings may be used here. Appropriate development rules and quality assurance processes ensure that each technical usage can be installed and operated independently.

Figure 2.6 shows the ABAP software components of enhancement package 4 for the product instance SAP ECC Server. Besides the underlying ABAP software components of the Application Server (AS) ABAP, this figure also shows the new SAP Business Suite software components *SAP Business Suite Foundation* (SAP_BS_FND) and *SAP Web UI Framework* (WEBCUIF). These new software components are also part of other applications of SAP Business Suite; for example, SAP Customer Relationship Management (CRM) and SAP Supplier Relationship Management (SRM). The software components are presented according to their dependencies to other software components. For a better overview, not all dependencies are included in the figure. By selecting the technical usage during the installation of the enhancement package, you can determine which software components are updated.

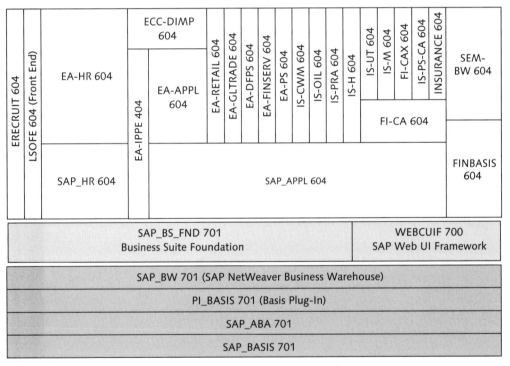

Figure 2.6 Overview of All Enhancement Package 4 ABAP Software Components (SAP ECC Server)

Besides the installable groupings of software components that are mapped via technical usages, there are some other rules for selecting software components to be installed. For example, an installed enhancement package version of a software component must be updated when another software component from a higher enhancement package version is installed. The following two examples illustrate possible target states of the SAP ECC Server after installation:

▶ **Example 1: Installation of Technical Usage Central Applications**
The software components that are highlighted in dark gray in Figure 2.7 were updated with the corresponding enhancement package 4 version in the SAP ERP 6.0 system.

▶ **Example 2: Installation of Technical Usage Human Capital Management**
The software components that are highlighted in dark gray in Figure 2.8 were updated with the corresponding enhancement package 4 version in the SAP ERP 6.0 system.

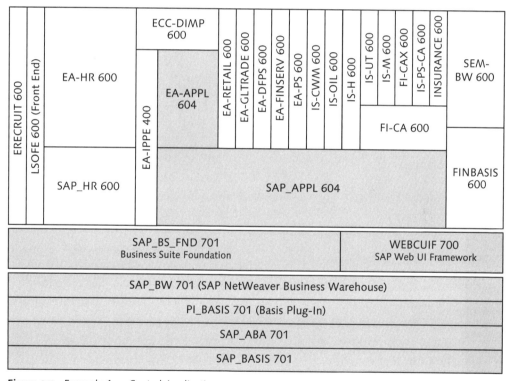

Figure 2.7 Example 1 — Central Applications

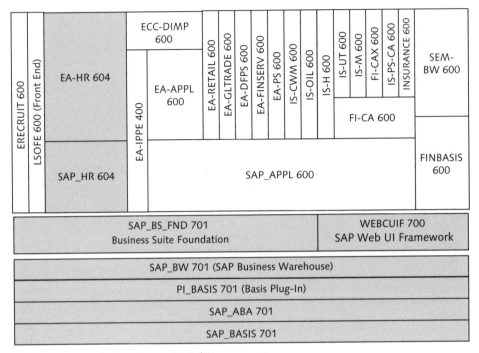

Figure 2.8 Example 2 — Human Capital Management

2.2.3 Prerequisites for the Installation of an Enhancement Package

An enhancement package, or a version of a software component is included in an enhancement package, can only be installed if specific prerequisites are met. Previously, we mentioned that an enhancement package enhances the underlying version of a product. From this, you can derive that at least the initial version must already be installed. Because SAP enhancement packages are developed to be functionally cumulative, the previous version of an enhancement package must also be installed (or integrated with the installation). For example, enhancement package 4 is based on enhancement package 3; the latter must therefore already be installed or integrated with the installation.

However, there are additional conditions that must be met for installation:

▸ **Support package level**
Because the software components to be installed can be freely selected to a large extent, a specific Support Package Stack is required from the software components that remain on the level of the underlying basis release; this is

important to support corrections across software components. For this reason, the support packages of the enhancement package and the support packages of the underlying basis release are synchronized. (Section 2.2.6, Support Package Strategy and Equivalence Levels, provides more details on this topic.) In the case of a comprehensive correction, it is therefore possible that one part of the correction is provided to the customer system in a support package of the underlying basis release, and the other part with a new version of a software component that is contained in the enhancement package.

▶ **SAP NetWeaver version**
Many functions of enhancement package 4 for SAP ERP are built on new SAP NetWeaver functions; that is, a specific version of SAP NetWeaver must be installed. For example, enhancement package 4 for SAP ERP partly depends on SAP NetWeaver enhancement package 1, which for example must be integrated with the installation for SAP ECC Server in either case.

Further import prerequisites can result from an enhancement package itself, because specific software components are based on other ones or because not all combinations of software component versions can be supported (see Section 2.2.1, Technical Usages and Product Instances). The *Maintenance Optimizer* automatically considers all prerequisites mentioned and integrates the required support packages or software components with the installation.

2.2.4   Cumulative Delivery

Enhancement packages follow a cumulative delivery concept; that is, an enhancement package version contains all business functions of the already-delivered enhancement packages. From a technical point of view, however, an enhancement package only contains the delta of the previous version. The interdependency with the previous version ensures that the business functions that have accumulated in all enhancement packages are imported. Therefore, the enhancement package 4 version of a software component is based on the enhancement package 3 version of the same component; for example, the SAP_APPL 604 software component is based on SAP_APPL 603.

The installation tools determine whether the enhancement package 3 version is already installed in the system or not; if it already exists, you only need to install the enhancement package 4 version that includes the delta of enhancement package 4 for enhancement package 3. If the enhancement package 3 version is not installed yet, it is automatically added to the list of component versions to be installed. Also, between the individual enhancement package versions, new business functions must be deliberately switched on. This ensures that only the already-activated functionality remains active after the import of enhancement packages into a system that already includes activated business functions.

If a business function that is new to enhancement package 4 (BF4) requires a business function from enhancement package 3 (BF3), this is ensured via a dependency between BF4 in enhancement package 4 and BF3 in enhancement package 3. In this case, BF3 can be independently activated at any time, while BF4 can only be activated if BF3 is already active, or if it is added to the same activation list. Dependencies of business functions on other business functions are visualized in the Switch Framework (see Section 2.3.1, Switch Framework). Additionally, the Switch Framework automatically checks to see if all dependencies are met and prevents activation if they are not.

2.2.5   Comparing Standard Release, Enhancement Package, and Support Package

During lectures and discussions on enhancement packages, customers often ask about the difference between delivery technologies, *upgrades*, *enhancement packages*, and *support packages*. Let's discuss these differences. To illustrate the difference between an enhancement package and a standard release or a support package, the following list compares them based on ten criteria:

1. **Key characteristics**
   What are the main characteristics of a standard release, an enhancement package, and a support package?

   ▶ **Standard release:** A standard release is a version of an SAP product where all software components belonging to the product are included in a version that was specifically developed for this release. An upgrade to a new standard release therefore entails the exchange of all software components belonging to the respective product, and also usually the software components of SAP NetWeaver. Examples of standard releases are SAP R/3 3.1I, SAP R/3 4.6C, SAP R/3 Enterprise Extension Set 2.00, and SAP ERP 6.0.

   ▶ **Enhancement package:** An enhancement package is a collection of software component versions that can be optionally installed. An enhancement package is always based on a specific standard release, and includes functional enhancements for this standard release. This special standard release is referred to as the *underlying basis release*.

▶ **Support package:** Support packages include quality improvements for the SAP system or implement necessary adaptations; for example, due to statutory changes. Support packages are provided specifically for a certain version of a software component. Therefore, there are support packages for software component versions from a standard release and for software component versions from an enhancement package.

2. **Main area of use**

For which type of changes are standard releases, enhancement packages, and support packages used?

▶ **Standard release:** To deliver new functionality and changes to existing functionality, you usually require a standard release. Besides the aforementioned functional changes, this can also include updates and changes to the software design. It also comprises the current corrections to existing functionality and adaptations of the software due to statutory changes.

▶ **Enhancement package:** Enhancement packages are specifically used for new, optional functionality and further developments of existing functionality. Enhancement packages always entail the installation of corrections and software adaptations due to statutory changes.

▶ **Support package:** Corrections to existing functionality and software adaptations due to statutory changes are provided via support packages.

3. **Compatibility with the previous version**

Is strict compatibility with the previous version ensured?

▶ **Standard release:** In a standard release, the focus is not on strict compatibility with the previous version; there can be major changes to the user interfaces and business processes that require additional user training. There can also be incompatible changes on the technical side, to a certain extent. For example, interfaces of function modules and methods or the design of applications or database tables can change. However, these changes are indicated explicitly, and a tool support can be provided if application data must be implemented. A new standard release usually entails functional changes in the application that affects users.

▶ **Enhancement package:** For an enhancement package, the compatibility with the underlying basis release plays a very critical role. For example, no changes to the user interfaces and business processes occur if the new functionality is not switched on. Exceptions are adaptations that are enforced due to statutory changes or error corrections. Also on the technical side, an enhancement package is mostly compatible with the underlying basis release so that no complex data conversions are required during installation. Only after the activation of new functionality can changes to the user interfaces, business processes, and interfaces occur, which can partly be incompatible.

Example: Treasury Migration

With SAP R/3 Enterprise 2.00, the architecture of inventory management in the treasury area was fundamentally changed, insofar as it was then possible to update parallel depreciation areas. Prior to SAP R/3 Enterprise 2.00, you could only update derived depreciation areas from the operative depreciation area. A change of the operative depreciation area, for example, from HGB (Handelsgesetzbuch; German Commercial Law) to International Financial Reporting Standards (IFRS), was not possible. This change in the architecture required a migration and thus an initialization of all depreciation areas if customers implemented a release change to this or a higher release.

▶ **Support package:** Incompatible changes — for example, deleting objects or renaming parameters — are generally not permitted, unless a correction or a statutory change makes it absolutely necessary.

4. **Installation prerequisites**
   What are the prerequisites for installation?

   ▶ **Standard release:** For the installation of a standard release, none of the prerequisites considered here must be met; at least not for a new installation. For an upgrade to a new standard release, however, at least the currently existing support package version must be considered. The new standard release's support package stack that corresponds to this (or a higher) version must be integrated with the upgrade procedure.

   ▶ **Enhancement package:** An enhancement package is based on a specific standard release. This specific standard release, a predefined support package version, and all already-available enhancement packages for the underlying standard release are automatically integrated with the installation if they are not already installed.

   ▶ **Support package:** A support package is based on a specific version of a software component. This version of the software component (regardless of whether it was integrated into the system with a standard release or an enhancement package) and all already-available support packages for this version of the software component must be available (or integrated with the installation).

5. **Effort for modification and enhancement adjustment**
   How elaborate is the adjustment of modifications and enhancements?

   ▸ **Standard release:** All software components contained in the product are replaced with all development objects. So this is a complete replacement where all modified objects must be handled accordingly (modification adjustment using Transaction SPAU).

   ▸ **Enhancement package:** The software components to be installed can be selected customer-specifically, with some restrictions. Only the objects changed by the enhancement package are replaced in the software components selected. So the expected adjustment effort is lower than for an upgrade to a new standard release. Moreover, the effort can be reduced in a targeted manner by only installing specific software components.

   ▸ **Support package:** The software components for which a support package is supposed to be installed can be selected customer-specifically, with some restrictions. However, we recommend that you import support packages within the scope of a support package stack. A support package only contains the actually changed objects; therefore, the potential adjustment effort is restricted to these objects.

6. **Implementation effort**
   How complex is the implementation of the new functionality?

   ▸ **Standard release:** Naturally, the effort for upgrading to a new standard release is usually higher than for implementing an enhancement package. Functional changes and cleansing that cannot be switched (and therefore are not immediately effective after the installation), and changes to the software design, increase the upgrade projects' costs for adjustments, tests, and trainings.

   ▸ **Enhancement package:** With regard to the implementation effort, an enhancement package has three major benefits when compared to a standard release. Because customers don't need to use the new functionality directly after the installation, the implementation effort does not occur until they are activated. So the first benefit is the separation between the installation and the implementation of the new functionality. The next benefit is that new functionality is provided in the form of business functions that can be switched independently of each other; you can explicitly decide which business functions are made available to which end user groups and when. For this reason, it is also possible to import enhancement packages as part of maintenance; that is, together with support packages. This way, the test and adjustment efforts occur only once. The third benefit results from the information, documentations, and test case templates provided for a business function, which describe in detail what is changed and what needs to be tested accordingly. Directly after the installation of an enhancement package, you can determine the costs for adjusting modifications and enhancements of the installed software components. As with support packages, enhancement packages only deliver the objects that were actually changed, and adjustment efforts can arise only for these. In addition to the adjustment efforts, expenses arise for tests (regression tests), which are usually within the budget for support packages.

▶ **Support package:** For a support package, the question about the training costs is not prevalent, because it usually doesn't contain any new functionality; only in the case of statutory changes can costs arise for user training. The implementation effort is restricted to the adjustment of modifications and enhancements and the test effort usually required for support packages.

7. **Maintenance**

For how long is maintenance provided?

▶ **Standard release:** A standard release is always a separate product version with its own support packages. Therefore, it is usually maintained according to SAP's known 7-2 strategy; that is, for seven years with the option to extend for another two years (see also *service.sap.com/maintenancestrategy*).

▶ **Enhancement package:** Each enhancement package is always a separate product version with its own support packages. An enhancement package is usually maintained as long as the underlying basis release.

▶ **Support package:** A support package (at least in the ABAP area) doesn't constitute a new product version, but contains corrections for a specific product version and is therefore not maintained as such.

8. **Selected activation of functionality**

Can new or changed functionality be switched on explicitly and optionally?

▶ **Standard release:** New functionality is usually available right after the upgrade. You are not always able to activate changes to existing functionality separately; they often take effect right after the installation. You can use customizing and configuration to influence the behavior and to also determine when new functionality becomes available.

▶ **Enhancement package:** You can explicitly activate all new functions or changes. The existing functionality remains unchanged without such an activation. The corrections included in the enhancement package are handled as delivered in the support package.

▶ **Support package:** The corrections included in the support package are delivered in such a way that they take effect right after installation. An explicit activation is not required. Only in the case of more complex corrections or statutory changes can new configuration options that have the same effects as activations arise.

9. **Type of switches used**

   Which technical type of switch is used to switch on the functional changes?

▶ **Standard release:** In standard releases, the Switch Framework has only been used in industry solutions. The regular application configuration is mainly done using the Implementation Guide (IMG).

▶ **Enhancement package:** The Switch Framework is used comprehensively in enhancement packages. New functionality and changes to existing functionality are provided in the form of business functions, which are part of the Switch Framework. Once a specific business function has been activated, this may require additional activities in the IMG.

▶ **Support package:** Switches are not usually required here. However, if you must correct an already-activated function, you use an already-existing switch. As mentioned previously, comprehensive corrections or statutory changes may necessitate additional steps in the IMG.

10. **Changes to user interfaces and processes**

    Can changes to user interfaces and business processes be switched?

▶ **Standard release:** Direct changes to user interfaces or processes can also occur in larger scopes.

▶ **Enhancement package:** Like every new or changed function, changes to user interfaces or business processes are always provided in a switchable form so that they only take effect when they are switched on.

▶ **Support package:** Switches are not usually required for changes to user interfaces or processes. However, if you must correct a business function that already depends on a switch, the correction is linked with this switch and only takes effect when the switch is active.

2.2.6 Support Package Strategy and Equivalence Levels

To better understand the maintenance of an SAP ERP 6.0 system using installed enhancement packages, this chapter describes the functioning of the equivalence principle between the support packages of different product versions.

Each enhancement package entails a new product version with separate support packages. You must synchronize the support packages of enhancement packages with the support packages of the underlying basis release. This way, you support comprehensive corrections in software components. This is particularly important, because not all software components of a system must have the same version.

SAP provides *Support Package Stacks* (SPS) as coordinated corrections for the software components of a product version. The initial version of an enhancement package also contains enhancements of the underlying basis release, and all corrections that are contained in the corresponding support package of this release (and still relevant in the enhancement package). This is also referred to as *equivalence support packages* or *equivalence maintenance levels*.

Example

The following Support Packages (SPs) of the different versions of the EA-APPL software component are equivalent with regard to the maintenance level:

► EA-APPL 604 SP01

► EA-APPL 603 SP03

► EA-APPL 602 SP04

► EA-APPL 600 SP14

Figure 2.9 illustrates the context. Each of the four versions of the EA-APPL software component comes from a different product version. The four product versions are shown as horizontal bars in the figure, where the four versions of EA-APPL and their support packages are displayed with an offset (to indicate the time sequence). The vertical bars indicate the previously mentioned support packages of the different product versions that have an equivalent maintenance level.

When installing an enhancement package, you must consider the equivalence principle in two ways: It determines the version of the support packages of software components that remain in the version of the basis release, and it determines the version of the support package of the enhancement package to be installed that must be integrated with the installation.

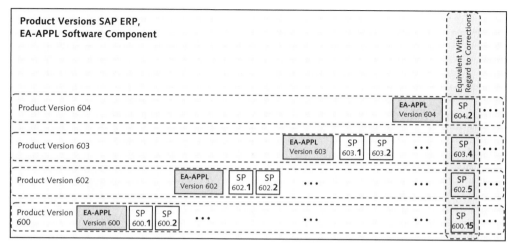

Figure 2.9 Equivalence Principle

The following are examples of the effect of the equivalence principle:

▶ To install enhancement package 4 (SPS1), the software components that remain in the SAP ERP 6.0 must have SPS14.

▶ If the basis is SAP ERP 6.0 with SPS15, the appropriate SPS2 must be integrated for the installation of enhancement package 4 (see Figure 2.9). This is necessary to avoid "losing" any corrections that are already included in SPS15.

The following rule of thumb always applies: For enhancement package installation, SAP Solution Manager's Maintenance Optimizer automatically determines the required packages that must be integrated with the installation.

To support this equivalence principle, SAP has synchronized the provision of enhancement packages and the provision of the corresponding support package stacks of the underlying basis release to a large extent. Whenever a new enhancement package or a new support package is released, a corresponding equivalence support package is determined and an appropriate support package stack of the underlying basis release is provided. Figure 2.10 summarizes the facts discussed so far:

▶ Each enhancement package is a new product version.

▶ Each product version is provided with separate support packages.

▶ The support packages of the different product versions are synchronized and correspond to the equivalence state.

▶ The SAP ERP enhancement packages are based on specific SAP NetWeaver support packages or on specific SAP NetWeaver enhancement packages.

▶ The equivalence support packages for an SAP ERP enhancement package are based on the corresponding SAP NetWeaver equivalence support packages of the respective SAP NetWeaver product version.

> **Note**
>
> The SAP NetWeaver enhancement packages also generate new SAP NetWeaver product versions, and equivalence levels also exist for SAP NetWeaver support packages. The latter two are not included in the figure for reasons of clarity.

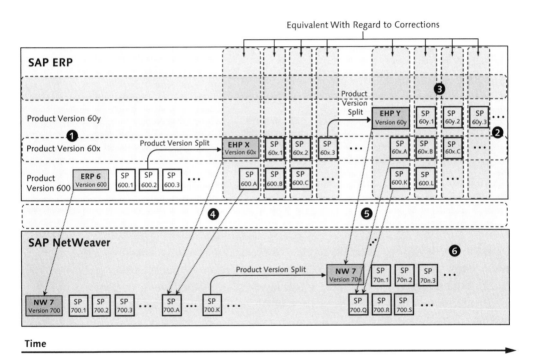

Figure 2.10 Example of the Equivalence Principle

2.2.7 Enhancement Packages for SAP NetWeaver

Enhancement packages for SAP NetWeaver can, in some ways, be compared to enhancement packages for SAP ERP; for example, both types of enhancement packages offer a new approach to delivering developments faster. But because SAP NetWeaver is an integration platform and serves as the basis for SAP applications such as SAP ERP, there are differences with regard to the enhancement packages of SAP Business Suite. SAP NetWeaver enhancement packages hardly ever provide the option to activate changes via business functions (one of these options is, for example, the *Periodic Key Replacement for Payment Card Encryption* business function, PCA_KEYV). User interfaces are usually activated with alternative means in SAP NetWeaver; for example, through configuration. Interfaces for administrators or developers can also be subject to nonactivated changes.

2.3 Development of Enhancement Packages

This section discusses the special requirements that arise in the development phase of an enhancement package and how they are built within SAP. The first part (Section 2.3.1 and Section 2.3.2, Enhancement Framework) present the technical basis of enhancement package development, including the *Switch Framework* and the *Enhancement Framework*. The second part (Section 2.3.3, SAP Enhancement Package Development Guidelines) answers the question of how these frameworks are used for an implementation of the enhancement package functionality.

To ensure that the installation of an enhancement package doesn't automatically cause any changes to the user interfaces or business processes, all changes or further developments must be developed as "switchable" — meaning that every change or development becomes effective depending on a switch. This is an essential change in the development process since SAP ERP 6.0, which affects all involved areas in development. The technical infrastructure consists of the Switch Framework and the Enhancement Framework, which are briefly presented in the following sections.

2.3.1 Switch Framework

The Switch Framework was first used with different industry solutions in the standard SAP ERP delivery (see Section 2.1, Brief Introduction to the Development of the SAP ERP Architecture). Now, virtually all industry solutions are included in the standard delivery, but they don't become visible or effective until an industry solution is switched on. This ability to hide certain objects and changes and make them visible or effective by means of a switch process is also used for enhancement packages. Here, all changes that directly affect user interfaces or business processes are offered as switchable.

Technical Components

The Switch Framework consists of three main components: the business function sets, the business functions, and the switches:

1. **Business function sets**

    Business function sets are primarily used for industry solutions. They group business functions that belong to a specific industry solution — the *industry business functions* — and are often also referred to as *industry business function sets*. In a system, only one business function set can be switched on; thus, it's impossible to use industry business functions from different industry solutions in a system that was implemented as a business function set. However, there are also industries that were not mapped using business function sets, and there are industry-independent parts of business function sets. In these cases, you can also use business functions of different industries in a system. Additionally, there are also business function sets that can be operated in one system at the same time. To map this, special business function sets are modeled that include the industry business functions of the combined business function sets. The OIL_&_GAS_WITH_UTILITIES business function set is an example here. It combines the two business function sets, OIL_&_GAS and UTILITIES.

    A general business function set exists in addition to the different industry-specific business function sets; it is used in the background to group the business functions of standard applications (Accounting, FI, HR, Logistics, and so on); these business functions are delivered in enhancement packages. These are referred to as *enterprise business functions*.

2. **Business functions**

    From a business perspective, a business function represents an independent business function that you can usually switch on independent of other business functions from the same enhancement package. From a technical perspective, a business function is a group of switches that are used to assign "switchable objects" to the business function. Business functions can be switched on in a system using Transaction SFW5, but they cannot be switched off again (as of enhancement package 4). Section 2.4.2, Reversibility of Business Functions, provides more details on switching off business functions. The following is a list of different types of business functions:

▶ **Enterprise extensions:** This type is also referred to as a *first-generation business function,* and is hardly ever used today. Enterprise extensions represent the extensions implemented with SAP R/3 Enterprise (SAP R/3 4.7), such as *SAP R/3 Enterprise Human Resource & Travel Extension 2.00.* They were integrated with the implementation of the Switch Framework, and they used to have a different technical basis. Enterprise extensions switch a multitude of industry-independent and industry-specific applications and business processes. They can be found in Transaction SFW5 in a separate folder called ENTERPRISE_EXTENSIONS.

▶ **Enterprise business functions:** These business functions are used for industry-independent functions of an enhancement package. They are used both by general industry-independent areas of SAP and by industry solutions. The latter only occurs if industry-independent functionality occurs within an industry solution, and this functionality can be used independent of an industry business function set. The enterprise business functions can be found in Transaction SFW5 in a separate folder called ENTERPRISE_BUSINESS_FUNCTIONS.

▶ **Industry business functions:** These business functions include functions that belong to the industry solutions that were returned with SAP ERP 6.0 (see Section 2.1. The industry business functions are part of the industry business function sets, and can only be used if the corresponding industry business function set is switched on. Today, they are still used for most enhancement package developments of industry solutions.

3. **Switch:** Business functions can be switched on, but they cannot switch ABAP development objects. Therefore, technical switches exist between business functions and development objects; you can assign objects to these technical switches either directly or via the package belonging to the development object. A switch can be "attached" to multiple business functions, and it is switched on as soon as a business function assigned to it is switched on. By activating a switch, you also activate the development objects assigned to the switch; in

other words, a switch groups a set of development objects that can be switched on *jointly*. Figure 2.11 illustrates the relation of business function sets, business functions, switches, and assigned switchable development objects.

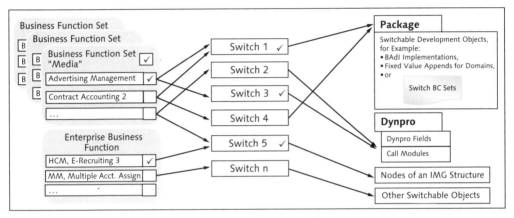

Figure 2.11 Relation of Business Functions, Switches, and Objects

Operation

Switches, business functions, and business function sets are independent, transportable units that you can manage using Transactions SFW1, SFW2, and SFW3. To switch on a business function, however, you only need Transaction SFW5. Transactions SFW1, SFW2, and SFW3, by contrast, are relevant if you need customized switches or business functions for customer developments.

Business functions with a gray bulb icon on the left (which are "switched off") can still be switched on provided that this is permitted by the respective dependencies (Figure 2.12). Such dependencies, which usually exist with other business functions, are indicated with a corresponding icon (⬚) in the DEPENDENCIES column. You can view the details by clicking on this icon. If all conditions are met and the business function can be switched on, the icon is changed (⬚).

The actual activation of the objects is done using a background job, which is automatically started by switching on business functions in Transaction SFW5. The job is called `SFW_ACTIVATE_SFOX` and it executes the `SFW_ACTIVATION_IN_BACKGROUND` report.

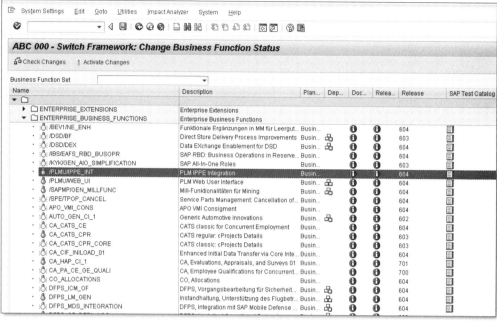

Figure 2.12 Activating Business Functions

Once this background job has been completed successfully, the extended functional scope is available. You can view the activation logs in Transaction SFW5 by following the GOTO • SWITCH FRAMEWORK LOGS menu path.

Business functions and, therefore, switches, are always switched across the system; as a result, a switch can never have different switch statuses in the various clients of a system. Currently, business functions and business function sets cannot be switched off again (see Section 2.4.2). So if you switch on business functions without due consideration, the worst case would be that you have to set up a system anew to restore the switched-off initial status of the business functions.

The installation of enhancement packages or support packages doesn't influence the switch statuses. All previously activated business function sets, business functions, and switches remain active. Furthermore, SAP doesn't implement any functional extensions for a delivered business function, which ensures that the previously active functionality can still be used, even after the installation of a support package or an enhancement package. Functional extensions of already-delivered business functions are provided in another business function that presupposes the first one; this ensures that — if required — only the functionality contained in the first enhancement package can be used after the installation of multiple enhancement packages.

2.3.2 Enhancement Framework

The Enhancement Framework is ABAP Workbench's new enhancement concept (first introduced with SAP NetWeaver 7.0). It is used to integrate different concepts to modify and enhance development objects. The goal of the new enhancement concept is to standardize all options that go beyond customizing, to modify or enhance SAP products (more precisely, repository objects of AS ABAP). The tool is called the *Enhancement Builder,* which is integrated with the ABAP Workbench. You can switch on, and therefore activate, the enhancements supported by the Enhancement Framework using the Switch Framework. Therefore, an enhancement is active when the package to which it belongs is assigned to a switch of the Switch Framework and this switch is switched on. You also utilize this connection of switch and Enhancement Framework for enhancement package development (for more details, refer to Section 2.3.3, SAP Enhancement Package Development Guidelines).

Central Entities of the Enhancement Framework

The enhancement concept of the Enhancement Framework comprises enhancement options, enhancement spots, and enhancement implementations. The following list discusses these in more detail:

▶ **Enhancement options**
Enhancement options are locations in repository objects where you can implement enhancements. These options are either defined explicitly — that is, predefined by a developer — or they always exist implicitly. You usually define *explicit enhancement options* in a central source system. Enhancements are made in target systems; that is, in customer systems, for example. The most important explicit enhancement options include *Business Add-Ins* (BAdIs) and enhancement points or enhancement sections. You use BAdIs to create predefined enhancement options in the source code, which can then be implemented by the individual industry solutions, country variants, and particularly by partners and customers as required. Enhancement points and enhancement sections are inserted directly in the source code using ABAP statements that are intended

specifically for this purpose. You can use source code plug-ins to enhance or replace the source code sections marked this way.

Implicit enhancement options exist, for example, in interfaces of function modules, which you can enhance with parameters, or at the beginning or end of ABAP programs where you can add source code.

▶ **Enhancement spots**
Enhancement spots are used for managing explicit enhancement options. They include information on the spots in the source code where enhancement options were created. You can manage multiple enhancement options of a repository object via an enhancement spot.

▶ **Enhancement implementation**
An enhancement implementation describes the enhancement of a repository object with one or more enhancement options, and consists of enhancement implementation elements. They always belong to exactly one enhancement option. However, multiple enhancement implementation elements can be assigned to an enhancement option. The enhancement implementation element contains the actual enhancement (for example, a source code plug-in contains the source code to be supplemented).

While implicit *enhancement options* always exist and don't require any special management, explicit enhancement options must be made known to the developers, who are supposed to implement them, via *enhancement spots*. Accordingly, enhancements that are implemented by developers must be managed as *enhancement implementations*. This applies to all enhancement options; that is, both for implicit and for explicit enhancement options.

Switchable ABAP Development Objects

It is important to know that not all ABAP development objects can actually be switched. For example, programs as a whole cannot be switched; changes to their source code, however, can be switched. The assignment of nonswitchable objects to switches has no effect. The corresponding objects are still visible and act as if they were not assigned to any switch.

Table 2.1 shows an overview of the most essential switchable ABAP development objects that can be switched via their assignment to a *package*.

Development Object	For What?
Append structures, includes, and customizing includes	Structures in the ABAP Dictionary
Append search helps	Search helps in the ABAP Dictionary
Secondary indexes	Database tables in the ABAP Dictionary
Fixed value appends	Domains in the ABAP Dictionary
Business configuration sets	Customizing
Enhancement implementations	Enhancement technologies of the Enhancement Framework, specifically implementations of BAdIs or other enhancement options

Table 2.1 Switchability via Package Assignment

Table 2.2 includes an overview of the ABAP development objects that can be switched by assigning them *directly* to a switch.

Development Object	How?
Dynpro field	A switch can be assigned to each dynpro field when it is defined in the Screen Painter. A dynpro field can only be used or is only visible if the assigned switch is switched on.
Call modules	The MODULE statement of the dynpro flow logic can be directly connected with a switch. Such a MODULE statement is only considered if the assigned switch is switched on.
Function codes	A switch can be assigned to a function code when it is defined in the Menu Painter.
Maintenance views and view clusters	A switch can be assigned to each field of a maintenance view in its definition in the ABAP Dictionary. This also applies to view clusters. For each view, you can specify a switch to control the visibility of the view.
Nodes of an IMG structure	A switch can be assigned to each node of an IMG structure in the IMG structure maintenance. An IMG structure node is only displayed if the assigned switch is switched on.
Nodes of an area menu	A switch can be assigned to each node of an area menu in the area menu maintenance. An area menu node is only displayed if the assigned switch is switched on.

Table 2.2 Direct Switchability

2.3.3 SAP Enhancement Package Development Guidelines

To ensure the characteristics of an enhancement package, the implementation of the new functionality must follow specific techniques and rules. The following sections describe how these techniques and rules were implemented by SAP within the scope of enhancement packages for the central development objects, considering the different aspects of such an implementation.

ABAP Source Code

ABAP source code is adapted or enhanced within the scope of developing enhancement packages to implement new functionality. (You can find a general introduction to the implementation of ABAP source code in the book *Object-Oriented Programming with ABAP Objects* by James Wood, SAP PRESS, 2009.) In the ABAP source code, you must ensure that the existing functionality is not changed until the activation of a business function. There are various enhancement mechanisms, and the technique used to implement the new functionality in the source code depends on whether or not the enhancement is in the same software component as the initial functionality.

One essential question is whether the enhancements exist explicitly or whether they must be created explicitly by changing the original source code. In the latter case, the source code object is delivered in a changed form; therefore this source code object occurs within the scope of the modification adjustment (see Section 2.2.3, Prerequisites for the Installation of an Enhancement Package). Figure 2.13 shows the different enhancement techniques that are used in enhancement packages.

Following is an overview of possible enhancement options:

► **Kernel-based BAdIs**
Kernel-based BAdIs represent a transparent and stable enhancement option. On the one hand, they have the advantage of providing a clearly defined interface that is kept stable. On the other hand, this technique enables the enhancement across software component boundaries. For this reason, this technique is basically used for enhancements that provide an industry solution in an enhancement package, and which you use to enhance the standard functionality. This involves an explicit enhancement technique because the option to call the BAdI doesn't need to be created until the initial source code.

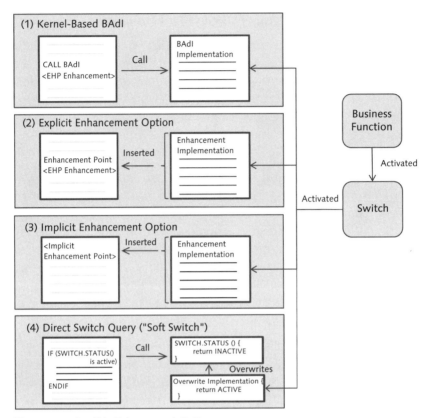

Figure 2.13 Possible Enhancement Options

▶ **Explicit enhancement options**

As described in Section 2.3.1, Switch Framework, you have the option of defining enhancement options in the ABAP source code. For these options, you can provide implementations that are added to the standard source code depending on the activation of a business function. The assignment of the enhancement implementation is done via the assignment of the implementation to a package, which in turn is assigned to a switch. The main difference when compared to the use of BAdIs is that there is no defined interface; the enhancement option must be added to the original source text using an ABAP statement (hence "explicit").

▶ **Implicit enhancement options**

Implicit enhancement options are automatically provided by the ABAP server. They exist in different predefined source code locations; for example, at the beginning or the end of a function module. In contrast to the other enhancement techniques, this involves a technique that doesn't presuppose any changes to the original source code (hence "implicit").

▶ **Direct switch query ("soft switch")**
A switch-dependent enhancement of source code can be achieved by controlling the execution of the corresponding enhancement source text via an IF condition. Here, the switch status is checked at runtime as the condition for executing the enhancement source code. The benefit of this procedure is that the source code that provides the enhanced functionality is also visible in the original source code. This makes it easier to gain an overview of the functionality. This also involves an explicit technique in which the original source code is changed explicitly.

To ensure the navigation from the switch to the source code passages that are influenced by the switch, the query of the switch status is implemented via a class method. They return the status of a specific switch (they always have the FALSE value in the standard implementation), and a switch-dependent overwrite implementation is created for this class method. This implementation returns the value TRUE and it is attached to the corresponding switch via its package assignment. So if the appropriate switch is switched off, only the standard implementation is active and returns the value FALSE. In the case of a switched-on switch, the overwrite implementation is active and returns the value TRUE, which results in the execution of the enhancement source code that is controlled via the IF condition.

Data Dictionary

SAP handles changes to the Data Dictionary Objects (DDIC) restrictively in enhancement package development. Incompatible changes — for example, the deletion or truncation of fields from structures and database tables — are prohibited. New fields are inserted at the end of existing structures and database tables. This prevents all types of changes that require manual or automatic adaptations or data conversions (for example, new after-import methods).

New secondary indexes, new elementary search helps in a collective search help, new views in a view cluster, and new fields in a maintenance view are delivered as switchable so that the changes do not become effective until a business function is switched on. This enables you to carry out the installation and implementation of an enhancement package as simply as possible. However, SAP delivers changes to the structures and database tables as not switchable. Even though this would be possible technically, structures and database tables play such a central role in

ABAP development that the comprehensive use of switchable elements would have resulted in major challenges due to the increased complexity. Structures and database tables that depend on switches are no longer stable in the sense of being unchangeable, but they are variable in their form. Every user would have had to respond to this variability appropriately and support each characteristic accordingly; that is, all usages of switched structures and database tables would have had to be implemented as switchable too. Source code that, for example, uses different structures that are each enhanced by different switches, would be difficult to understand, and error-prone. Nevertheless, changes to the structures and database tables cannot directly affect the interfaces and business processes. In this context, the "users" — that is, the locations in the source code that use these structures and database tables — play a significant role. In these locations, the missing interconnection is compensated by appropriate measures of these DDIC changes.

ABAP Dynpro and Web Dynpro ABAP

For all user interfaces that are changed by SAP within the scope of an enhancement package, the rule applies that these changes must not become visible until the activation of a business function. For the main technologies, ABAP Dynpro and Web Dynpro ABAP, you are provided with a direct integration with the Switch and Enhancement Framework:

▶ **ABAP Dynpro**
The visibility of ABAP Dynpro fields and the execution of dynpro flow logic modules can be assigned to switch directly via the Switch Framework (in the development environment). The changes to the dynpro do not become effective until the switch is activated.

▶ **Web Dynpro ABAP**
Web Dynpro ABAP is integrated with the Enhancement Framework and allows for the switch-dependent enhancement of Web Dynpro ABAP applications. Such enhancements are not implemented in the change mode, but in the enhancement mode that is specifically provided for this purpose. All changes that are made this way are part of an enhancement implementation, and they become part of the actual Web Dynpro ABAP application when the enhancement implementation is activated.

Table Entries

Table entries that are provided by SAP can also influence processes or user interfaces. To ensure that this does not occur directly during the import of an enhancement package but during the activation of a business function, these table entries aren't delivered directly but are bundled in *Switch Business Configuration (BC) Sets*. Switch BC Sets are transportable containers that can contain table entries and are assigned to a switch via their package. A Switch BC Set is not unpacked until the assigned switch is activated, and the table entries contained therein are added to the appropriate tables.

Non-ABAP

Enhancement packages not only provide new functionality for the ABAP server, but also include new or changed Java applications, and content for SAP NetWeaver Portal, SAP NetWeaver BW, or SAP NetWeaver PI. The characteristics of enhancement packages also apply for these non-ABAP parts. Here, it is important that you can install ABAP backend and non-ABAP parts independent of each other. All existing processes continue to run without any changes if an enhancement package is only installed in parts of a system landscape. You only need to import and activate the appropriate ABAP and non-ABAP parts if new business functions are supposed to be used. In this case, the technical usage that is assigned to the business function includes both ABAP and non-ABAP parts.

Thus, product deliveries of SAP Business Suite not only comprise ABAP-based applications but also some applications that are written in Java. The enhancement package principles also apply for these applications: They ensure that no direct changes occur when a new version is imported. In principle, Java-based applications can be subdivided into two categories, each of which is handled differently:

▶ **Java applications that are closely coupled with an ABAP backend and do not provide their own business logic.**
Frequently, these involve pure user interface applications. Here, the activation status of the business function in the ABAP backend is the indicator that the Java application uses to provide new functionality. The Java application automatically determines the activation status from the corresponding backend system.

▶ **Java applications that provide their own business logic.**
These applications usually contain a configuration that is available via the Java server. Within the scope of an enhancement package delivery, a new configuration parameter is added that activates the new functionality. The Java application evaluates this parameter accordingly. So the new parameter ensures that the application's behavior does not change after the installation.

Portal Content

Portal content comprises roles and role parts that are used via SAP NetWeaver Portal. They are loaded to the *Portal Content Directory* (PCD) during installation, are assigned to users or user groups, and allow for user-specific access to systems. The main part is a structured menu of the different applications.

Because the system displays the portal content directly to the user, it must not change after the import of an enhancement package version. This is ensured by implementing each change within a new portal role in a new namespace. This way, the existing role is not changed, and no changes arise for the users of the original role. The new role version does not become active until it is assigned to a user.

Business Intelligence (BI) Content

BI content objects for SAP NetWeaver BW are only partly switchable, but they can be influenced by switches in the appropriate backend. New or changed BI content objects are available in an inactive form in the *BI content repository* after the import and after the administrator activates them explicitly. This ensures that no changes to the used BI evaluations arise after the import of a new BI content version. When you activate the new BI content or the assigned business function, you must then consider the interdependencies. These are described in the appropriate documentation.

PI Content

Enterprise services belong to those objects that are only partly switchable. Their visibility is not influenced by switches, but their behavior can be. This means that a new enterprise service is visible immediately after the installation of the corresponding technical usage, just like changes to the already-existing enterprise services are visible immediately after installation.

However, the behavior of an enterprise service depends on the called source code, which in turn can depend on switches. Without further measures, this would be an unfavorable situation: The enhanced interface of an enterprise service or the existence of a new enterprise service can give the impression that the service in its present form can be used independent of all switches and business functions. But this is only the case if the service's source code doesn't depend on any switch. For this reason, all enterprise services that can only be used if specific switches are switched on contain a special check for this purpose. In the case of an error, the process is canceled with a corresponding error message. Additionally, it is defined in the documentation of the enterprise services whether a dependency exists for a business function.

2.3.4 Effects on Customer Developments

As described previously, enhancement packages not only entail the delivery of new development objects, but also changes to existing development objects. The change is designed in such a way that it doesn't affect the processes directly; from a technical perspective, however, it represents a change of the original object. So the object is delivered in a changed form. When it is imported to a customer's system, it is subject to the same processes as any other changed object.

A modification adjustment is necessary, particularly if the object was modified in a customer's system. This is done via the standard modification adjustment using Transaction SPAU. In addition to the changes to the original objects, the delivery of the enhancement packages also includes enhancement implementations that are integrated from the ABAP generation into the original source code upon their activation. Because these enhancement implementations become part of the original source code, this may result in conflicts between a modification of the original source code and the enhancement implementation. The same applies if an enhancement implementation was modified and the original source code is changed. You handle these conflicts using Transaction SPAU_ENH, which uses the same principle as the regular modification adjustment.

2.4 Business Functions

Business functions are the central unit of enhancement packages. They are used to determine the installation units and control the activation of the functions as described in Section 2.2, Architecture of Enhancement Packages, and Section 2.3. In addition, business functions provide additional functions and utilities, which are described in the following sections.

2.4.1 Change Analysis of the User Interfaces (Impact Analyzer)

As was already described earlier in this chapter, the user interfaces and processes initially don't change for the end user after installing enhancement packages. Among other things, this avoids needing user training right after the installation, because training can take place later on when the business functions are activated. Moreover, the training is restricted to the area that the business function affects.

To facilitate the planning of this user training, you can use the Impact Analyzer (Transaction SFW5) to get information about which user interfaces are changed during the activation of a specific business function (Figure 2.14). The result list contains the following information:

▶ Transactions, reports, and Web Dynpro ABAP applications, whose user interfaces change when a business function is activated

▶ User roles to which these applications are assigned

▶ Users to which the corresponding roles are assigned

You can obtain an initial estimation of the amount of training this way.

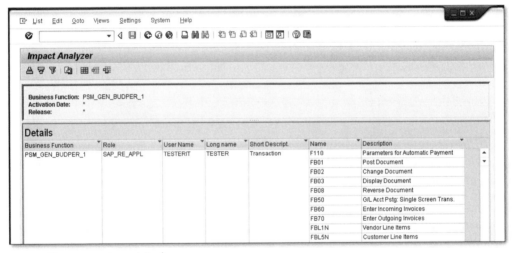

Figure 2.14 Impact Analyzer

2.4.2 Reversibility of Business Functions

Up to and including enhancement package 4, you cannot deactivate business functions again. For this reason, the activation of a business function must be considered carefully. You should get information about its scope (in the documentation and the release information) and analyze its impacts on certain user interfaces (Impact Analyzer); you should only activate the business function when you are sure that you want to implement the changes.

The only way to comprehensively test a business function and then potentially not use it is to use a separate test or sandbox system (see Chapter 3, Successful Enhancement Package Project Management). However, in the future, SAP may also provide some reversible business functions; these could then be deactivated in the development and quality assurance system under specific technical conditions. Moreover, this would enable testing of a business function without a special sandbox system before the business function is used in production.

2.4.3 Transport of Switch Statuses in System Landscapes

Business functions don't need to be activated separately and manually in every system; you can use a transport to copy the statuses of the business functions of one system to another system. Note that you always transport the statuses of *all* business functions existing in the system in this process. This function is available via Transaction SFW5 (or via the menu path: SYSTEM SETTINGS • TRANSPORT), as illustrated in Figure 2.15.

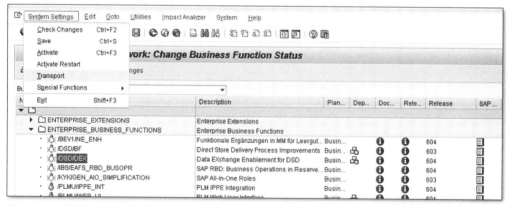

Figure 2.15   Transport in the Switch Framework

Figure 2.16 shows the use of the transport function within the system landscape. This procedure — that is, the exclusive use of the transport function — ensures that the same business functions are activated in development systems (DEV), in quality assurance systems (QAS), and in production systems (PRD). Therefore, the same conditions apply in the systems mentioned, which is indispensable for a representative test in the quality assurance system.

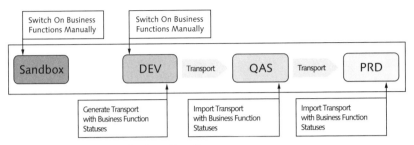

Figure 2.16 Transporting Business Functions

2.4.4 Documentation and Test Case Templates

The documentation and the release information for business functions ensure that all functional changes and their impacts on the business processes and user interfaces are known or can be assessed before the business function is activated. By means of *test case templates* for business functions, you can reduce the actual time required for the implementation of a business function and the resulting costs.

You can download the documentation, release information, and test case templates prior to the installation of an enhancement package from the Enhancement Package Info Center (*http://service.sap.com/erp-ehp*) in the SAP Service Marketplace. After installing an enhancement package, the information for each business function is also available via Transaction SFW5. For more information, refer to Section 4.6.6, Test Catalogs and Test Case Templates.

Documentation and Release Information

The documentation and release information in Transaction SFW5 of the Switch Framework describe the functional scope of a business function and its possible uses (Figure 2.17). They provide an overview of the most critical changes to the user interface and processes, and of the Customizing activities that may be necessary after activating a business function. Additionally, a reference to the corresponding APPLICATION HELP is provided for each new function.

This way, the application expert can clarify the business function's impacts on the system prior to its activation. He can evaluate which Business Function should be used within the enterprise or the individual user departments, and which should not. He can also assess and plan the scope of user delta trainings. Application experts and administrators can use the information about the technical features and preconditions of a business function to check whether all preconditions are met, or whether additional activities or preparations are necessary to use a business function.

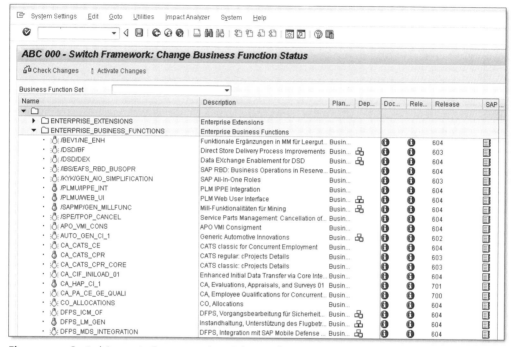

Figure 2.17 Central Access to Documentation, Release Information, and the SAP Test Catalog

Test Case Templates

Templates for test cases are available for the business functions that are delivered with enhancement packages. You can use these templates to test new functions of a business function, and therefore reduce the duration and costs of the implementation. The use of test case templates offers the following benefits:

▶ The test case description contains information on how you can test new functions and what you need to consider in this context.

▶ Test case templates can be supplemented with further test cases.

▶ You can plan upcoming tests based on the test case templates; the costs can be calculated.

▶ Tests can be prepared with regard to content; for example, by creating the necessary test data.

Therefore, test case templates have the scope of an *acceptance test*, which is used to determine whether the new functionality meets the special requirements and expectations of the customer. However, they are not a complete *regression test*, which is usually implemented after the installation of a support package stack and after the installation of an enhancement package. Therefore, they don't cover the corrections and statutory changes included in an enhancement package.

2.4.5 Business Process Change Analyzer

SAP Business Suite customers, who want to use the Business Functions of enhancement packages to implement new functions for their SAP solution, ask themselves which critical business processes will be affected by activating the business functions. It is critical to subject these business processes to targeted functional tests and regression tests before the new business functions are activated in the production landscape.

SAP Solution Manager 7.0 enhancement package 1 offers the *Business Process Change Analyzer* (BPCA) tool to generally analyze the impacts of software changes on business processes. SAP plans to enhance the BPCA, shown in Figure 2.18, to identify business processes that are affected by the activation of business functions. The following sections describe the technical procedure.

Preparatory Measures

A precise and customer-specific impact analysis of business processes by the BPCA assumes that there is a list of the business processes' technical objects to be analyzed. To create this list, users can use SAP Solution Manager's BPCA to start and execute these business processes without any special technical knowledge. The BPCA records all used SAP objects (user interfaces, program code, customer enhancements, function modules, table accesses, and so on) in the background. These objects are then assigned to the respective business process in the *SAP Solution Manager Blueprint*.

Alternatively, you can use automated tests; for example, *extended Computer-Aided Test Tool* (eCATT) or HP *Quick Test Professional* (QTP), to automatically record the *Technical Bill of Material* (T-BOM). You can find examples for the creation of suitable automated tests on the additional information page at *http://service.sap.com/testing*.

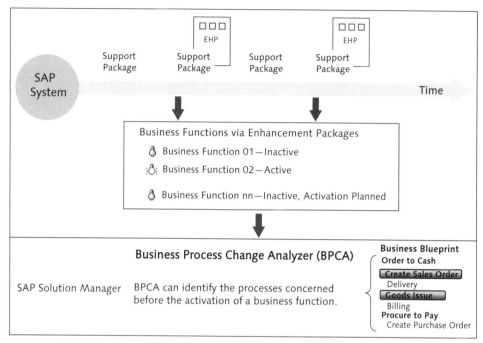

Figure 2.18 BPCA

Moreover, the customer must have the relevant enhancement package that includes the not-yet-activated business functions installed. The connected SAP ERP system must also have a specific SP level for enhancement package 4 to implement the business function analysis.

Implementing the Analysis

The BPCA has started using the Planned Business Function Activation option, which enables the user to select one or more business functions that are not yet activated. As already described, the quantity of available business functions is determined by the imported enhancement packages. Another start option refers to the business processes to be analyzed, which are grouped by SAP Solution Manager projects or solutions.

After the analysis has been started, the customer receives a reference number that the various users can use to call the analysis results. The BPCA allows for a multi-level analysis with the following details:

▶ SAP Solution Manager projects or solutions and the business processes contained therein that would be affected by a subsequent activation.

▶ For each business process or process step, the analysis lists the SAP objects that are reprocessed if the selected business function is activated.

▶ SAP customers who have manual or automatic test cases that are managed in SAP Solution Manager can generate a test plan with all of the test cases from the display of the analysis results to enable a regression test of the business processes concerned.

Customer Benefit

The new preview function of the BPCA provides the following benefits for SAP customers:

▶ Overview of the business processes that are affected by the planned activation of business functions. The analysis is *prior* to a business function's activation, which is irreversible in many cases.

▶ SAP customers can use the analysis results as a basis to assess the scope of the regression tests required.

▶ Based on the assignment of test cases to business processes in SAP Solution Manager, customers can generate a test plan for the regression test.

This chapter introduces you to the project-related aspects of enhancement packages. It explains all of the relevant phases and activities. A real-life example and useful tips are also included.

3 Successful Enhancement Package Project Management

Whereas Chapter 2, Architecture and Technology, focused on the architectural and technical aspects of enhancement packages, this chapter describes the project aspects. This book uses the *Application Lifecycle Management* (ALM) approach as the basis for planning and implementing enhancement package projects. The Application Lifecycle Management approach also serves as the basis for the mapping of technical and application-specific activities, which are introduced in Section 3.2, Application Lifecycle Management.

3.1 Five Success Factors for Enhancement Package Projects

Before turning to these details, let's first look at an overview of the five success factors of enhancement package projects. If the following aspects have been planned and organized in detail, the success of the project is "only" a question of a professional implementation of the activities that are described in Section 3.3, Enhancement Package Project Phases and Activities.

3.1.1 Maintenance Planning

Most SAP customers define the maintenance schedule of their system landscape in their annual IT planning. For SAP systems, this means that fixed dates for the import of support packages are already scheduled. As described in Chapter 1, Introduction, the required parts of the current SAP enhancement package should be included in this maintenance activity. You must consider the following aspects when planning maintenance activities:

▶ **Optionality**

Are new functions required? If you can answer this question with a clear no, you don't have to import an enhancement package.

▶ **Selectivity**

Which functions are required? The following rule of thumb applies: Avoid a full installation! A full installation of SAP enhancement packages has a negative effect on the runtime and downtime, and usually doesn't provide functional added value. For example, the majority of industry solutions exclude one another during activation, because only one industry business function set can be activated per system. Because only one enhancement package version is permitted per system, a full installation provides an additional disadvantage: A customer who wants to implement new business functions of enhancement package 4 and already has a full installation of enhancement package 3 in his SAP ERP system must therefore also install enhancement package 4 completely. A combination of an old and a new enhancement package version is not allowed.

In real life, however, it is possible to separate the implementation of business planning and information technology (IT) planning. This alternative approach enables the IT department to update the used (that is, relevant) parts of the SAP ERP Central Component (ECC) server with an enhancement package.

Here, all parties involved must understand how much additional effort beyond the support package update is required for the enhancement package installation. The system administrator, for example, needs time to become acquainted with the new tool for the enhancement package installation, *EHP Installer*.

Ultimately, the enhancement package project must correspond to the IT strategy and the projects of the customer that are planned in parallel to achieve the greatest synergy possible. You also have to consider the effects of the enhancement package projects in this context; for example, the impact of blocking the development environment for parallel projects during the installation.

Recommendation

▶ Evaluate, at an early stage, if and which content of the currently available enhancement package is supposed to be used.

▶ The next time you maintain the system, import the respective parts of the enhancement package together with the support packages.

▶ Plan your time realistically.

3.1.2   IT Infrastructure Planning

Detailed and early infrastructure planning is a basic prerequisite for a successful enhancement package project. This section focuses on the required compatibility checks and the correct technical sizing of the systems.

Compatibility

Every enhancement package supports the latest version of the operating systems and databases at the time of the package release. Here, SAP allows for specific combinations of operating systems and databases. Older enhancement packages (for example, enhancement package 2 for SAP ERP 6.0) may still be available for platforms that are no longer supported by the respective provider. Prior to the project's start, you should therefore check whether the current enhancement package is available for your currently used IT platform (database and operating system).

SAP centrally documents these prerequisites in the *Product Availability Matrix* (PAM) at *http://service.sap.com/pam*. Here, you can find information on supported operating systems and databases, and on available country versions and languages of the corresponding application.

Technical Dependencies

The second aspect that needs to be checked is the dependencies within the system landscape. The *Upgrade Dependency Analyzer* (UDA) supports you in analyzing technical compatibilities within the SAP system landscape. You can access it in the SAP Service Marketplace at *http://service.sap.com/uda*.

To check non-SAP products and add-ons for compatibility, you have to contact the respective manufacturer to clarify if the corresponding package is allowed for these products. For SAP add-ons, you can check SAP Note 1226284 to see if enhancement package 4 can be used for a respective add-on.

Sizing

In general, enhancement packages up to version 3 do not require additional system resources after the technical installation. Along with enhancement package 4, SAP Note 1311835 was released. It indicates a very low additional requirement for main memory and CPU, which have to be considered accordingly. The additional requirement for processor performance, memory, and memory space is currently 0% to 5%. When using new functions in production, you still have to use the Quicksizer or refer to the Sizing Guidelines (which you can find at *http://www.service.sap.com/sizing*) to determine additional hardware requirements.

Unicode

In general, the same rules apply to enhancement packages that apply to the underlying basic release (SAP ERP 6.0). Therefore, you can install enhancement packages in Unicode and in single code page systems. SAP Notes 79991 and 838402 provide further information on this topic.

> **Recommendation**
>
> Check prior to the start of the project to see if your system meets the following requirements:
>
> ▸ Platform (operating system and database)
>
> ▸ Additionally required hardware
>
> ▸ Connected systems and interfaces

3.1.3 Necessary Adjustment Work

Adjustment work is usually necessary after installing enhancement packages. One of the reasons for this is that most customers work with a SAP system that is adapted to their requirements, which entails modifications, enhancements, and customer-specific developments. In addition, existing objects are replaced during the installation. Although this, as described in Chapter 1, Introduction, and Chapter 2, Architecture and Technology, has no effect on the end user, because the user interfaces remain unchanged, it still affects the required postprocessing tasks.

For example, if you use a strongly adapted system with numerous modifications, it makes sense to test the enhancement package installation as soon as possible in a test or sandbox environment. This lets you identify important findings at an early stage; for example, the required effort for the adaptation tasks and if the SAP enhancements are compatible with your own developments. During or after installation, you are provided with a list of the SAP objects that need to be adjusted and can be processed using familiar transactions, Transactions SPDD and SPAU. Another benefit of the sandbox installation is that your Basis administrators can gain important experiences with EHP Installer.

This procedure is also critical for evaluating the installation runtime and the technical downtime at an early stage. For more information on this approach, refer to Section 3.1.4, Change Management — Sandbox System and Double Maintenance. The following section describes the most important tasks that have to be performed within the scope of the necessary adaptation work.

Modifications

Modifications are changes to repository objects in the SAP namespace. The import of new versions of existing SAP objects can lead to conflicts with the modified SAP objects. Basically, there are two alternatives: Either you return to the SAP standard or you keep the modification (that is, you also implement the modification for the new SAP object).

The modification adjustment is part of every system update with support packages or enhancement packages. You analyze and process modifications to Data Dictionary Objects (DDIC) using Transaction SPDD. Conflicts with DDIC objects must be handled very carefully, because errors can have severe consequences. In the worst case, data will be lost and inconsistencies will occur within the system.

Conflicts with repository objects are analyzed and processed using Transaction SPAU. To minimize the effort, you should regularly check the rate of capacity utilization of modified and self-developed objects (how often has a program or transaction actually been called by the end users?). This can be done, for example, on the basis of performance statistics via Transaction ST03. Another valuable approach is to ask whether particular modifications or custom developments can be replaced using (new) standard SAP functions ("back to the SAP standard").

Customer Developments

Developments in the customer namespace are not directly affected by enhancement package installation. They remain as they are. Nevertheless, depending on the type of the custom developments, postprocessing can be necessary. One of the reasons for this is the use of SAP-specific objects in customer developments (*cloned objects*). Chapter 2, Section 2.3.3, Enhancement Package Development Guidelines of SAP, explains how SAP implemented enhancements for various object types and follow-on activities that may result for the customer. In the worst case, SAP code has been copied and further processed in the customer namespace (which should not be done). Here, the risk for complex postprocessing is particularly high, because the integration with other SAP objects is usually very close. In this case, you should also manually check which custom developments are still used and which developments are no longer needed (for example, via Transaction ST03). An adaptation that is restricted to the programs and objects actually used reduces the effort significantly. The utilization analysis is also supported by special tools in SAP Solution Manager.

> **Recommendation**
>
> ▸ Assign development resources as support for the enhancement package project.
> ▸ The further away the system is from the SAP standard, the higher the adaptation effort. Consider the effort accordingly.
> ▸ For substantially modified systems, a sandbox installation is useful, because it enables you to evaluate and consider the adaptation effort at an early stage.

3.1.4 Change Management — Sandbox System and Double Maintenance

Most enterprises have defined structured change management for existing systems. Change management describes how functional requirements for the system are evaluated and how changes are then implemented and used in live operation. This established mechanism should be used when implementing enhancement packages. To start the installation, you must first assess the use of the new functionality (business function). Furthermore, you must identify potential side effects.

Using a Sandbox System

A sandbox installation is a good opportunity to evaluate the new functions in detail. Moreover, you can ensure that the activated business functions contain the desired enhancements.

Because activation of business functions is currently not reversible (see Chapter 2, Section 2.4.2, Reversibility of Business Functions), you can avoid making functional changes that are not recommended in the system landscape by using a sandbox system. This is only if a part of the business functions that are activated in the development system are also activated in the production system at a later stage; for example, if not all of the business functions are required. Figure 3.1 illustrates a possible system landscape with a sandbox system.

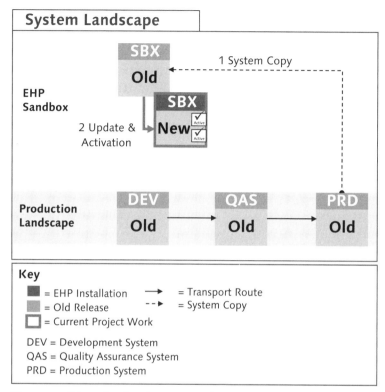

Figure 3.1 Using a Sandbox System to Evaluate New Business Functions and Detail the Project Planning

If the sandbox system is a copy of the production system, it has the following benefits:

▸ You can assess the resulting runtime and downtime at an early stage

▸ You can analyze and estimate the effort for the necessary postprocessing tasks (using Transactions SPDD and SPAU)

▸ Test data is available for initial business tests

The disadvantages are mainly the additional hardware and memory capacity requirements, and the fact that developments that are currently processed and cannot be transported to the production system cannot be analyzed. In the event of bottlenecks of the available hardware, you can copy the development system — but then you have to live with restrictions for the runtime estimation and application tests.

Organizing Code Freeze

After installing the enhancement package in the development system, the developers have to perform the respective adaptation tasks for the repository objects. To provide the existing production system with (emergency) corrections in a reasonable manner, it makes sense for long enhancement package projects to provide a copy of the original development system. In this case, you must ensure that the change is also maintained in the parallel development system with the same enhancement package status. Otherwise, the changes that have been transferred to the production system via the temporary maintenance system would be lost after the enhancement package installation in the production system, because the old development system will be disabled afterward.

The process of parallel maintenance of two development systems is also referred to as *double maintenance*. Here, the changes between the two development systems are usually transferred manually, because SAP recommends that you not use automatic transports between systems with different structures (for example, with different software component versions).

To reduce this effort to a minimum, you should provide for a *code freeze* throughout the duration of the enhancement package project. This is supposed to minimize the number of parallel changes (and thus minimize changes that need to be maintained twice). The only exceptions during the code freeze period are emergency corrections that would be directly transported to the production system via the temporary development system. In real life, it is often difficult to agree on a period of limited developments with the various user departments, because they fear that they respond to new requirements less flexibly during this period. It is therefore important to plan and communicate this phase early. Due to the short project duration, the code freeze should only last a few weeks for most customer projects anyway. A sandbox, in turn, can help you fulfill some prerequisites to further minimize the code freeze. For more information on cross-release transports, refer to SAP Note 1090842. The book, *SAP Change and Transport Management*, by Armin Kösegi and Rainer Nerding, SAP PRESS, 2009, also provides valuable background information on this topic. Figure 3.2 shows a possible system landscape with a maintenance system.

Business Downtime: Minimizing the Downtime

During the installation of enhancement packages, the production system is unavailable to the end user for several hours. Therefore, minimizing this downtime is an additional project task. This holds particularly true if the production system is critical and creates extra costs for every hour it is not available.

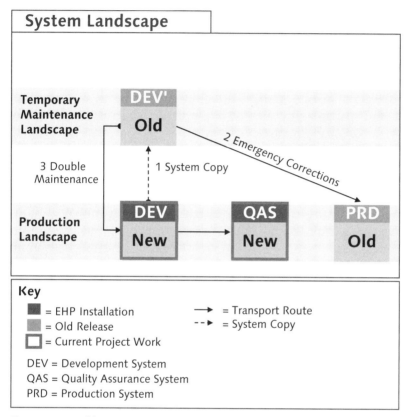

Figure 3.2 Double Maintenance Procedure in the System Landscape

As described in Chapter 4, Section 4.5.2, Development from the Repository Switch to the System Switch Procedure, you can reduce downtime if you use the system switch procedure for installing enhancement packages. A lot of the installation steps can thus be performed while the system is still in live operation.

To minimize business downtime, it is not sufficient to solely limit the technical activities of the installation tools, you also have to optimize the postprocessing. The most important activities during business downtime include:

▶ Ramp-down of the system (logging off users, shutting down interfaces, checking and, if required, emptying queues)

▶ Technical installation steps (technical downtime)

▶ Customer transports (repository, customizing, changes)

▶ Acceptance of the system by business (including tests)

▶ Ramp-up of the system

Usually, the installation process with EHP Installer is performed at least three times during an enhancement package project: in the development system, in the quality assurance system (QAS), and in the production system. Throughout this chapter, we've already mentioned some reasons for scheduling the creation of a sandbox system at an early stage. In this case, it can also make sense to use a sandbox system, because this lets you evaluate the runtime and downtime of the enhancement package installation in your customer-specific environment at an early stage.

You should document the individual steps to reuse the description of the customer-specific installation activities as a kind of "installation cookbook" for all subsequent updates (see Chapter 5, Section 5.2.2, Installation Cookbook). If you follow the instructions in the cookbook, and if the input parameters remain constant, you can improve the installation procedure with each update and thereby make sure that you will perform a smooth update of the production system.

If the tools' accumulated technical downtime doesn't meet your expectations, you should analyze the phases using the logs. Chapter 5, Section 5.3.2, Installation Runtime and Downtime, provides more details on analyses, downtime optimization, and customer statistics.

Recommendation

▶ Create a sandbox system at an early stage to make a qualified decision about using the new business functions.

▶ Weigh the advantages and disadvantages of using a temporary development system for emergency corrections.

▶ Consider using a temporary development system. In this case, you should ensure that new developments and enhancements are limited: Provide for a code freeze — that is, a phase in which no development or only limited development activities take place.

3.1.5 Test Management

The goal of all project activities is to resume operation without any problems after a successful go-live. To ensure this, a part of every maintenance project is to test support or enhancement packages. The key to success is to define the scope of the test appropriately. Because customers often have many custom developments and modifications in their systems, you should at least provide for a regression test, which ensures that all enterprise-critical core processes are tested. Usually, a regression test is the largest cost of an enhancement package project. The following distinctions have to be made for the test:

▶ At the very least, a regression test has to be carried out after the technical installation (without activation of the business functions).

▶ An individual test planning should be implemented after the activation of a business function using the SAP *test case templates*. Here, the test case templates describe recommended follow-up tests. You should also carry out an acceptance test with users.

▶ If the installation directly involves the activation of new functionality, you need to carry out a regression test and an acceptance test.

Improvements in the test environment and test management can have the greatest impact on the overall effort of an enhancement package project. Use SAP Solution Manager with its Test Workbench and the integrated test automation tool, eCATT.

The SAP standard for test management (*http://service.sap.com/supportstandards* • Media Library) provides all of the necessary information on the recommended test management procedures and tools available. The book, *Testing SAP Solutions*, by Markus Helfen, Michael Lauer, and Hans Martin Trauthwein, SAP PRESS, 2007, provides a detailed insight into the test topic.

Recommendation

▶ Carefully define the scope of the test, and take into account the legal requirements and your individual risk profile.

▶ At the very least, provide for a regression test after the installation.

3.2 Application Lifecycle Management

The underlying concept here is Application Lifecycle Management. Based on the generally accepted model of *IT Infrastructure Library* (ITIL), Application Lifecycle Management is divided into six phases (see Figure 3.3). Application Lifecycle Management of SAP is characterized by a holistic approach that not only includes the process-oriented use of tools but also addresses organizational aspects in consistent solution operation (*Customer Center of Expertise*), methods (*ASAP* and *Run SAP*), and *standards for E2E solution operations,* and the *SAP services portfolio*. Application Lifecycle Management covers the entire lifecycle of IT solutions.

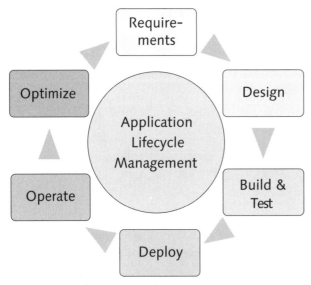

Figure 3.3 Application Lifecycle Management

This lifecycle includes the following six phases in compliance with ITIL:

▸ **Requirements**
Compilation of requirements for new applications or for the distribution of existing applications

▸ **Design**
Translation of the requirements into detailed specifications and planning of the technical aspects

▶ **Build & Test**
Implementation of installation, application configuration, and test activities

▶ **Deploy**
Transfer of all changes to the existing production IT landscape

▶ **Operate**
Provisioning of IT services that are required for continuous operation

▶ **Optimize**
Analysis of the service level fulfillment and possible start of actions for improving the results

Every Application Lifecycle Management phase is supported by integrated Application Lifecycle Management processes. For more information on Application Lifecycle Management, and particularly on the supported Application Lifecycle Management processes, navigate to the SAP Service Marketplace at *http://service.sap.com/alm* or to the SAP Community Network (SCN) at *http://www.sdn.sap.com/irj/sdn/alm.*

Innovation Management

Innovation management as an Application Lifecycle Management process refers to the identification of business requirements and the preparations necessary to implement them via collaborative processes. This process facilitates the alignment of new requirements with enhancements provided by SAP. Within the scope of SAP Business Suite 7, these enhancements are made available for all core applications through enhancement packages.

For the implementation of enhancement packages within the scope of innovation management, the first four Application Lifecycle Management phases are relevant, because they serve to describe the project's activities (see Figure 3.3). The phases *Operate* and *Optimize*, in turn, cover the operation and optimization of the solution. According to the enhancement packages concept, the technical installation can also be implemented as a part of the system maintenance decoupled from the functional enhancement. In this case, the new functionality would be activated in a second step. However, because the number of activities ultimately remains the same, you can describe the technical and functional aspects along the lifecycle together, thus providing a holistic picture without avoidable redundancies. There are also customers that use synergy effects for installing in real life (for example, in the test environment) and activate and implement initial business functions in a targeted manner during installation.

Therefore, this chapter provides a *combined* description, based on the Application Lifecycle Management approach, of the technical and functional implementation. If you're interested in the technically steps for a subsequent activation, Chapter 5, Section 5.4, Recommendations on Activating Business Functions, provides valuable information.

SAP Solution Manager Enterprise Edition is the basis for the consistent and efficient management of an application's lifecycle. You can find a detailed description of the SAP solution for Application Management and of the administration in the book, *SAP Solution Manager Enterprise Edition,* by Marc O. Schäfer and Matthias Melich, SAP PRESS, 2009.

The following descriptions concentrate on the four project phases, *Requirements, Design, Build & Test,* and *Deploy.* Usually, various teams and roles are involved in the process, and they usually belong to two core areas of the organization: to a specific user department and to the IT department (Figure 3.4).

> **Note**
>
> Please note that, in practice, the names and exact task distribution of the roles and areas can vary between one enterprise and the next.

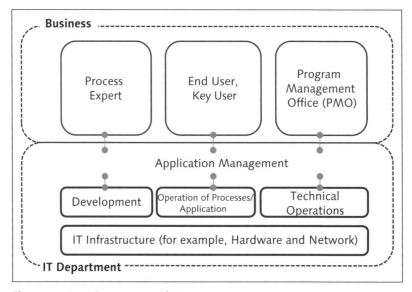

Figure 3.4 User Department and IT Department

Based on this model, the following describes the core tasks for the different groups of people:

▸ **Activities of the IT department**

▸ **Technical operation**
Administrators implement and ensure the technical operation of the SAP systems. Among other things, this includes installations, updates, upgrades, and the technical monitoring of the SAP systems.

▸ **Development**
Developers are usually responsible for customer-specific enhancements within the IT department.

▸ **Application support**
Application support is responsible for the definition of the processes and their configuration, and acts as the central interface between IT and user departments by gathering their requirements. Application support employees are in direct contact with various business areas and are ultimately responsible for the implementation of business requirements and end user support.

▸ **Process operation**
There is frequently an independent group that deals with the operation and monitoring of business processes and applications to ensure smooth production deployment.

▸ **Activities of the user department**

▸ **Program management office**
The business areas usually include a program management function that is used to centrally initiate and control programs.

▸ **Process experts**
Process experts are responsible for the definition of business requirements.

▸ **End users and key users**
These are the end users that work with SAP applications on a daily basis. Key users are experienced SAP end users that represent specific end user groups and usually have a multiplier function within the area.

Table 3.1 lists the most important roles, and their organization affiliations and tasks, in the context of enhancement package implementations.

Role	Organization	Tasks
Project manager	User department or application support	▸ Project management
Test coordinator	User department or application support	▸ Organizing and performing tests
Process expert	User department	▸ Designing the business processes ▸ Approving changes
Administrator	IT infrastructure or SAP Technical Operations	▸ Updating, maintaining, and operating SAP systems
Key user	User department	▸ Testing the business processes ▸ Supporting the go-live
Developer	Development	▸ Analyzing and implementing changes (development, data models, customizing if required)
Application support employee	Application support	▸ Defining the processes in coordination with the process experts ▸ Implementing the business requirements ▸ Configuration

Table 3.1 Central Roles and Tasks

3.3   Enhancement Package Project Phases and Activities

This section explains the flow of the required project activities, tasks, and results. Figure 3.5 provides an overview of the interaction between the various parties involved, and their main activities along the four enhancement package project phases. The activities for the creation of the business case for new functions are optional.

3.3.1   Phase 1: Requirements

The goal of the *Requirements* phase is to evaluate the new functions and define the desired functional scope. The basis for this is the requirements of the user departments and IT department, which can be mapped to the enhancement package functions.

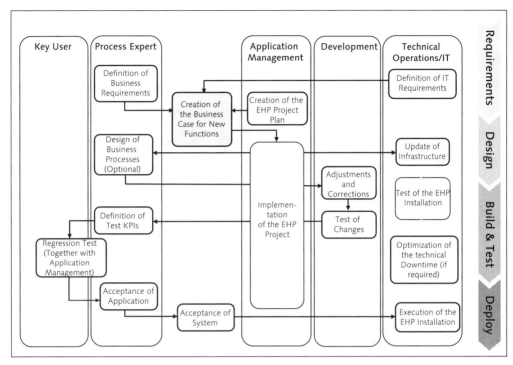

Figure 3.5 Overall Flow of the First Four Project Phases

Selecting the Required Business Functions

In the first step, the application enables employees and business process experts to analyze which business functions are required. They are provided with the necessary information through the following sources:

▶ **Enhancement Package Info Center**
The Enhancement Package Info Center in the SAP Service Marketplace (*http://service.sap.com/erp-ehp*) is the central access point to obtain all necessary information on the new business functions of enhancement packages. For example, here you can find overview presentations, online help, release information, and test case templates.

▶ **SAP support services for enhancement packages**
SAP provides service offers as a part of the enterprise support to impart deeper knowledge about enhancement packages and their content. This also includes the *Accelerated Innovation Enablement* remote service, in which SAP experts provide you with a functional and technical overview of the enhancement pack-

83

ages, and support you in the early planning phase. Chapter 4, Section 4.6.8, Service Offers for Enterprise Support Customers, provides more information on this service.

▶ **Solution browser tool**
The solution browser tool lets you search for delta functions between releases and SAP enhancement packages in a targeted manner (you can find additional information at *http://erp.fmpmedia.com* and Chapter 4, Section 4.6.3, Solution Browser Tool).

Figure 3.6 shows the enhancement package roadmap, which provides an overview of the basic enhancements of the enhancement packages that are available to date.

| | Q2 2007 | Q4 2007 | Q2 2008 | Q2 2009 |
	EHP1	EHP2	EHP3	EHP4
HCM	HR Shared Services	Talent Management: Learning	Talent Management: E-Recruiting	Talent Management: New User Experience
Financial Accounting	Credit and Collection	Bank Communication Management	Financial Statement	Treasury & Risk Management Master Data Governance
Process Optimization	Adaptive Manufacturing	Simplification of Sales Order Processing	Simplification of Procurement Process	Outsourced Manufacturing
Corporate Services		Simplification of Travel Management	Simplification of EH&S	Service Sourcing Recycling Administration

Figure 3.6 Roadmap of the Functional Enhancement Package Components

The scope of delivery of SAP enhancement packages also includes enterprise services. Bear in mind that the *ESA ECC-SE* technical usage only contains a part of the available enterprise services. Enterprise services are also available in other technical usages. For more detailed information on enterprise services, refer to the following:

- ▶ Enterprise Service Workplace at *http://esworkplace.sap.com*
- ▶ SAP Developer Network (SDN) at *www.sdn.sap.com* • N Service-Oriented Architecture • Explore Enterprise Services
- ▶ SAP Note 1359215

The result of the *Requirements* project phase is a list of desired business functions, which is forwarded to the technical administration. Only a list of the required business functions enables you to identify the parts (technical usages) of the enhancement package that need to be technically installed later on.

If possible, you can use a sandbox system to test and analyze the new business functions. For more information, refer to Section 3.1.4.

IT-Driven ("Broad") Installation as an Alternative

If the user departments cannot select an individual list of business functions, there is an alternative approach — at least for the SAP ECC Server. On the basis of the already-used functions in the SAP ERP system, the administrator selects the technical usages providing enhancements. For example, he would select the Human Capital Management technical usage for a human resources (HR) system. (We assume that the IT department knows the system's purpose, which is usually the case.) Chapter 5, Section 5.1.2, Practical Approach for Selecting Relevant Technical Usages, describes the procedure in detail.

However, this also indicates the disadvantage of the IT-driven installation: If completely new business functions are required (for example, if an HR system is supposed to be enriched with enhanced functionality; e-recruiting, for instance) that go beyond the current scope, you have to install them separately, which involves additional (subsequent) project input. Therefore, the general recommendation is still applicable: Evaluate the new business functions in advance, and subsequently install all required technical usages for the selected business functions.

SAP Enhancement Packages and Licenses

You don't need new licenses for a technical installation of enhancement packages for SAP ERP. However, before you activate business functions, keep this in mind: Regarding licenses, enhancement packages have the same behavior as release upgrades; they simply present a different delivery method. Among other things, SAP's software price concept is based on the number and type of users and on business key figures. This applies to functions in SAP ERP 6.0 and to enhancements and new functions that are delivered with enhancement packages. You can find details on SAP's price structure at *www.sap.com/solutions/licensingmodel/index.epx*. After having decided which functions from SAP ERP or from an SAP enhancement package you want to use, please contact your sales representative. He can provide you with detailed licensing information on the selected functionality.

Training

Basis administrators have to work with new SAP tools when you install enhancement packages. You should therefore check to see if you need to book a special training course for the administrators (for example, the ADM 327 course). The capabilities and competences of all project members are critical success factors for the project (you can find more information on trainings and courses at *http://sap.com/services/education*).

> **Result of Phase 1 — Requirements**
>
> You should compile a list of business function that cover the future demand of business and IT requirements. If this analysis is not feasible, but you still want to proactively provide the latest business functions, you should deploy the IT-driven approach. In this case, the result of the first phase is a list of technical usages.

3.3.2   Phase 2: Design

In the design phase, you plan the enhancement package installation with regard to technologies and functions. At the end of the phase, you have a detailed project plan that describes all of the necessary project activities.

The core of the project preparations are the factors that are discussed in Section 3.1, Five Success Factors for Enhancement Package Projects:

- ▶ Maintenance planning
- ▶ Infrastructure planning
- ▶ Application adaptation
- ▶ Change management
- ▶ Test management

Prerequisites

Ideally, you should check to see if all of the necessary prerequisites are met as early as possible. So, during the design phase, you can read the latest documentation on the selected enhancement package. For administrators, this also includes the *Enhancement Package Master Guide*, the installation guide, and the notes referenced therein.

An essential prerequisite for installing SAP enhancement packages for SAP ERP is SAP Solution Manager. Chapter 4, Implementation Tools and Service Offers, contains more details on the necessary preparations in SAP Solution Manager.

> **Note**
>
> In general, no minimum support package level is required for an enhancement package installation. The prerequisite support packages are part of the entire installation queue and can be installed in one technical step.
>
> Do not import support packages to your SAP ERP system immediately before an enhancement package project! This can lead to problems, because the equivalent support package stacks of initial and target state may not be immediately available from SAP.
>
> Moreover, to install support packages and enhancement packages separately is not useful. Enhancement packages always have a specific maintenance level (see Chapter 2, Section 2.2, Architecture of Enhancement Packages); thus, it is technically impossible to install the enhancement package without parts of the corrections from the support packages. This is another reason why you should import enhancement packages together with support packages. If you have only installed the support packages, it can negatively affect the technical runtime and downtime of the subsequent enhancement package installation. In such a case, you have to reperform a regression test with the usual developers' adaptation work; in other words, the project costs increase due to the unnecessary repetition of tasks.

Identifying the Technical Usages and Downloading the Packages

In the next step, the administrator must map the required business functions to the corresponding technical usages (*mapping process*). This is done with SAP Note 1165438, which clearly describes the mapping and indicates the technical packages (software components) for technical usage. The mapping of business functions and technical usages is detailed in Chapter 2, Section 2.2. Architecture of Enhancement Packages. Table 3.2 provides a brief overview of the PDF documents that are attached to SAP Note 1165438.

The required packages are determined and downloaded using the SAP Solution Manager Maintenance Optimizer. This tool guides the administrator through the preparation process by following a structured procedure. Chapter 4, Implementation Tools and Service Offers, provides details on the Maintenance Optimizer, and on the necessary maintenance of the system landscape in Transaction SMSY and in the *System Landscape Directory* (SLD).

File Name	Sorted By	Mapping To		
enhancement package4_ BF_TU_Mapping.pdf	Business functions	Technical usage	Product instance	Business packages (content)
enhancement package4_ TU_BF_Mapping.pdf	Technical usages	Business functions	Product instance	Business packages (content)
enhancement package4_ BF_SWCV_Mapping.pdf	ABAP-based product instances	ABAP-based enhancement package 4 software component versions		
	Java-based product instances	Java-based enhancement package 4 software component versions		

Table 3.2 Content of the Mapping Tables from SAP Note 1165438

Result of Phase 2 — Design

At the end of the phase, the project plan and all project members and their tasks should be defined. Furthermore, all necessary prerequisites should be met, and the test focus, the downtime requirements, and the temporary maintenance strategy of the production system should be specified.

3.3.3   Phase 3: Build & Test

In this phase, you implement the plan that was defined in the previous phase. Here, the enhancement package is downloaded using SAP Solution Manager. Afterward, it is installed with the latest support package on the development system. As of enhancement package 4 for SAP ERP, the administrator uses the new installation tool, EHP Installer, for the installation.

Technical Installation of Enhancement Packages

EHP Installer is based on the proven *system switch procedure* that is also used for upgrades. Here, a temporary shadow system is created in which most of the activities can be carried out; for example, the delta import or the activation of the objects. A benefit is the minimization of the technical downtime of the system.

You can find more on this in Chapter 4, Section 4.5, SAP EHP Installer. Make sure that you downloaded the latest EHP Installer version from the SAP Service Marketplace (*http://www.service.sap.com/ehp-inst*) at the beginning of the project. You should use this version to test and document the procedure. Figure 3.7 illustrates the installation process.

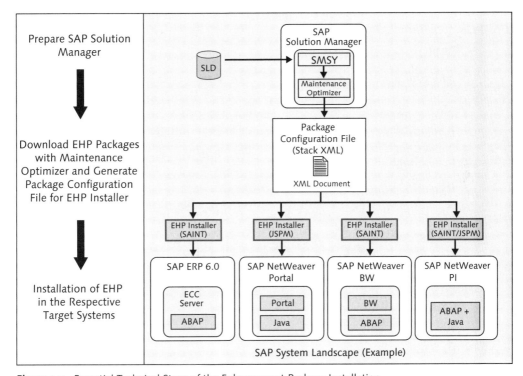

Figure 3.7 Essential Technical Steps of the Enhancement Package Installation

After the installation of the enhancement package in the development system, the developers need to adapt the modifications (using Transactions SPDD and SPAU; see Chapter 2, Section 2.3.3. After the QAS has been updated and the project transports have been imported, the process experts and, if required, the key users can carry out the regression test.

Activating the New Functionality in the Switch Framework

The last step in the enhancement package project is the activation of the business functions via the Switch Framework (Transaction SFW5). It is up to you if you want to activate the new functions immediately after the installation, or if you want to carry out a second project to do so. The following applies: If no switch is changed here, the functional behavior of the system doesn't change either. The activation of the business functions enables you to make new functions that are available within the SAP ERP system selectively visible for various end user groups. During activation, a job runs in the background that implements the necessary changes in the system. You therefore have to allocate technical downtime for the activation, at least for the areas affected. Bear in mind that the activation is currently irreversible. You can find further details in Chapter 2, Section 2.4.2, Reversibility of Business Functions.

In addition, there is the central *Switch Framework cockpit* in SAP Solution Manager Enterprise Edition (see Chapter 4, Section 4.6.7, Switch Framework Cockpit). This is the control center of the Switch Framework. It allows for a central control from SAP Solution Manager so that you don't have to call Transaction SFW5 in every single system. Prior to the activation, the Switch Framework provides all of the necessary information on the available business functions:

▶ **Online documentation**
The online help gives you an overview of the new functionality.

▶ **Release notes**
They describe the functional delta to the previous function.

▶ **Test Case Template (TCT)**
TCTs provide information on the necessary functional tests after activating a business function. Usually, an acceptance test is carried out with the end users after the activation.

▶ **UI Impact Analyzer**
Customers can use this tool to analyze the end-user-specific effects of the user interface changes after the activation of a business function.

▶ **Dependencies on other business functions**
The dependencies between business functions indicate, for example, if other business functions need to be activated as well, or if they exclude one another.

Chapter 2, Section 2.3, Development of Enhancement Packages, explains the function and use of the Switch Framework in detail.

Recommended Enhancement Package Project Landscape

This section describes a risk-minimized approach for building up your project landscape in the *Build & Test* phase. Note: There are variants for the design of a project landscape that primarily depend on the customer's requirements and options. For example, it is entirely possible that you don't need additional hardware in the project landscape for a small, uncritical production system. However, it is also possible that additional systems — for example, a temporary system for quality assurance — are used.

The following describes essential requirements in the risk-minimized project landscape for the *Build & Test* phase (see Figure 3.8):

1. A system copy of the current development system (DEV*) to have a system for creating emergency corrections for the production system throughout the project; this also initiates the optional code freeze and the double maintenance.

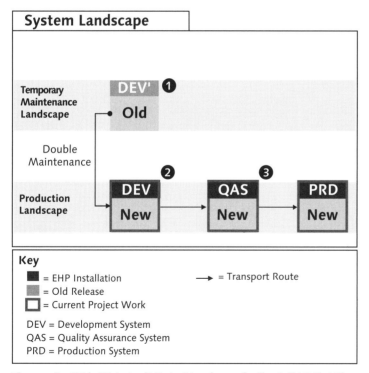

Figure 3.8 "Risk-Minimized" Project Landscape for the Build & Test Phase

2. Enhancement package installation in the development system (DEV):

  ▶ Adaptation work carried out by developers (Transactions SPDD and SPAU).

  ▶ If new functions are implemented directly, activate the selection business functions and their configuration.

3. Installation of enhancement package 4 in the QAS:

  ▶ Regression test carried out by application support employees and key users.

  ▶ If new functions are implemented directly, training and acceptance test are carried out by key users and end users.

Result of Phase 3 — Build & Test

At the end of the third phase, the enhancement package is in the development and QAS. The necessary work is completed, and the critical core processes have been tested successfully (regression test). If a business function has been activated, the corresponding configuration activities and an acceptance test have been carried out. During this time, the planned maintenance strategy for the production system (if required, with double maintenance and code freeze) is implemented.

3.3.4 Phase 4: Deploy

The goal of the *Deploy* phase is to update the production system and go live with the project. That is, this phase comprises the technical downtime of EHP Installer (you can find more details and statistics in Chapter 5, Section 5.3, Analysis and Optimization of an Enhancement Package Installation), and the necessary postprocessing activities within the business downtime.

The detailed cutover planning should encompass all project steps that have to be performed during the business downtime. After the final acceptance test, a decision is made about the go-live release of the SAP system landscape. You should also have a fallback plan in the case of a "no-go" decision. Once the "go" decision has been made, live operation is prepared and resumed. After the transition weekend, the core project team usually doesn't provide support for some days so that they can analyze and solve unexpected problems as soon as possible. The temporary SAP systems of the landscape are removed at the same time. The official project completion ends all project-related activities.

> **Result of Phase 4 — Deploy**
>
> The enhancement package installation (including downtime) was successfully implemented on the production system. Technical and expert postprocessing activities were carried out, including the final tests and subsequent release. In addition, end-user support was ensured after the go-live. Finally, all temporary systems were removed, and the project was completed.

3.4   Enhancement Package Project Statistics

The SAP Enhancement Package Experience Database (see Chapter 4, Section 4.6.2, SAP Enhancement Package Experience Database) provides statistics on completed enhancement package customer projects (via the SAP Service Marketplace at *http://service.sap.com/enhancementpackage-DB*). The following information is gathered there:

- Project duration
- Project input
- Satisfaction

This way, SAP provides benchmark data that provides you with initial clues and guidelines for planning an enhancement package project. However, the planning should always apply to your specific situation; that is, project duration and input may considerably deviate from the median value. You should therefore use the schedule of your last maintenance project as the basis for the enhancement package project planning. Figure 3.9 shows an overview of the influencing factors.

System and Landscape Complexity

In addition to the complexity in the system landscape (number of systems, interfaces, and so on), the complexity of the system itself is a central factor for determining the overall project input. As the number of modifications and custom developments increases, so does the effort for adaptations and tests.

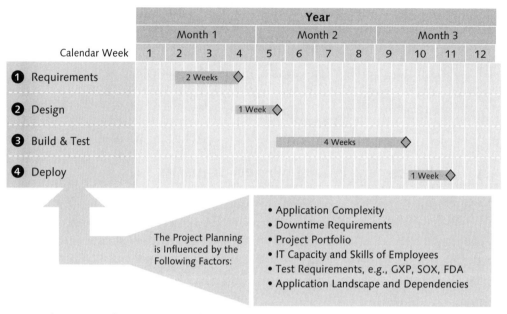

Figure 3.9 Influencing Factors of the Enhancement Package Implementation

Test Requirements

In some industries, such as chemicals and pharmaceuticals, comprehensive tests may be necessary due to legal regulations. Because testing is an essential cost of any maintenance and upgrade project, you can find more time-consuming and more complex projects in some industries. You must therefore consider the individually required test scenarios when planning your enhancement package project.

3.5   Customer Example

This section introduces an enhancement package 4 implementation project using a real-life customer example. Our sample enterprise is currently planning the next maintenance project of its SAP system landscape and wants to address the SAP enhancement packages topic within the scope of this maintenance project.

3.5.1   Project Idea

Concrete functional requirements in the e-recruiting area are planned for the next financial year, and additional functional requirements in the core area of the SAP

ERP 6.0 system (the SAP ECC Server) are likely. These requirements are supposed to be met with the enhancement package 4 installation. The new functions are not supposed to be switched on in the first project step; instead the focus is supposed to be on the technical provisioning of the new functions. Once the project is completed, selected business functions can be switched on in a sandbox system, and the content of the new functional scope must be evaluated. The project is planned according to the Application Lifecycle Management approach; as the basis for a detailed project plan, the schedule of the last maintenance project is to be used and complemented.

The Challenge

In previous maintenance projects, the corrections were always installed using the *Support Package Manager* (Transaction SPAM); however, for the installation of enhancement package 4, the EHP Installer tool is being used for the first time. An additional challenge is that all systems of the landscape are supposed to be provided with the enhancement package functionality at the same time, which increases the complexity and risk of the project. To meet these challenges, the customer plans to first test the technical installation on a sandbox landscape. The following factors have been defined for the project's success:

▶ Early specification of the technical requirements

▶ Consistent support from the user departments

▶ Evaluation of the technical installation process on sandbox systems

▶ Project-related technical consulting by SAP

▶ Use of SAP Solution Manager

3.5.2   SAP System Landscape

The SAP system landscape of the customer constantly follows a three-level approach and consists of development systems, QAS, and production systems. The systems are connected via transport routes within a system landscape line. This means that the SAP system landscape consists of three product lines:

▶ A three-level SAP ERP 6.0 landscape (SAP ECC Server) (ABAP-stack systems) with the following system IDs:

  ▶ DE1

  ▶ QE1

  ▶ PE1

- ▶ A three-level SAP NetWeaver Portal 6.0 landscape (Java-stack systems) with the following system IDs:
  - ▶ DP1
  - ▶ QP1
  - ▶ PP1
- ▶ A three-level SAP NetWeaver BW 7.0 landscape (dual-stack systems) with the following system IDs:
  - ▶ DB1
  - ▶ QB1
  - ▶ PB1

Figure 3.10 shows the customer's current SAP system landscape.

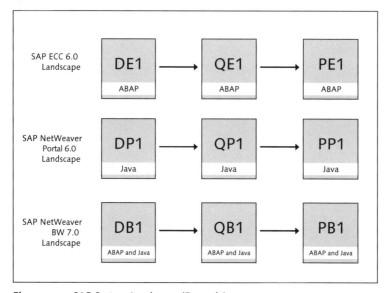

Figure 3.10 SAP System Landscape (Example)

3.5.3 Project Phases

The following sections describe the implementation of the project based on the Application Lifecycle Management method.

Phase 1: Requirements

In the *Requirements* project phase, the user department analyzes and determines the new functional requirements. The results of this project phase are forwarded to the Basis team in a table that contains the identified business functions (*see* Table 3.3).

No.	Business Function	Technical Name
1	HCM, SAP E-Recruiting – Search 1	HCM_ERC_SES_1
2	HCM, SAP E-Recruiting 1	HCM_ERC_CI_1
3	HCM, SAP E-Recruiting 2	HCM_ERC_CI_2
4	New General Ledger Accounting	FIN_GL_CI_1

Table 3.3 Identified Business Functions

Phase 2: Design

Table 3.4 provides the Basis team with the specifications on the technical usage that has been identified using the mapping report in SAP Note 1165438.

No.	Business Function	Technical Name	Technical Usage	Content
1	HCM, SAP E-Recruiting – Search 1	HCM_ERC_SES_1	ERecruiting on ECC Server	No
2	HCM, SAP E-Recruiting 1	HCM_ERC_CI_1	ERecruiting on ECC Server	No
3	HCM, SAP E-Recruiting 2	HCM_ERC_CI_2	ERecruiting on ECC Server	Yes (Portal Content: all business packages)
4	New General Ledger Accounting	FIN_GL_CI_1	Central Applications	Yes (BI Content: Yes)

Table 3.4 Supplementing the Identified Business Function with Technical Details

This analysis indicates a requirement of additional content in SAP NetWeaver Portal and SAP NetWeaver BW. The technical team uses this table to implement the maintenance project.

The following landscape options are possible:

- SAP ERP 6.0 landscape (SAP ECC)
  - Installation of enhancement package 4 with the currently available support packages
  - Installation tool: EHP Installer
- SAP NetWeaver Portal 6.0
  - Option A: installation of enhancement package 1 for SAP NetWeaver 7.0 (including support packages) and of Portal Content with the installation tool, EHP Installer
  - Option B: installation of the support packages and of Portal Content with the *Java Support Package Manager* (JSPM)
- SAP NetWeaver Business Warehouse (BW) 7.0
  - Option A: installation of enhancement package 1 for SAP NetWeaver 7.0 (including support packages) and of Business Intelligence (BI) Content with EHP Installer
  - Option B: installation of the support packages and of BI Content using Transaction SPAM (for the ABAP-stack system) or the Java Support Package Manager (for the Java-stack system)

Due to the new portal functions, the customer decides to install enhancement package 1 for SAP NetWeaver 7.0 on SAP NetWeaver Portal (option A). Only the latest support packages and BI Content are supposed to be installed on the SAP NetWeaver BW landscape (option B), because no additional technical requirements are necessary here. For more information on the enhancement package 1 content, see the SDN at *http://www.sdn.sap.com/irj/sdn/nw-70ehp1*.

This information is used to create the maintenance processes in SAP Solution Manager to generate the technical packages and stack XML files. The Basis team created a matrix for orientation purposes (see Figure 3.11). The following selection was made for the first maintenance process (SAP ECC and SAP NetWeaver Portal):

- Product version
  - Enhancement package 4 for SAP ERP 6.0/NetWeaver 7.01
- Technical usages
  - Central Application
  - ERecruiting on ECC server
  - Portal Content and Portal Content Common

The following selection was made for the second maintenance process (SAP NetWeaver BW):

▶ Product version

  ▶ SAP NetWeaver 7.0

▶ Additionally

  ▶ BI Content 704

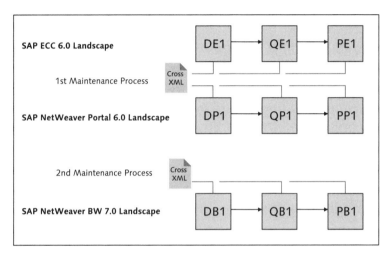

Figure 3.11 Generated Maintenance Processes

After the installation was completed, the customer detected that the accumulated enhancement package 4 sandbox installation downtime on SAP ERP 6.0 (SAP ECC Server) was too long and no longer within the available downtime window. After an analysis, factors were determined that will be corrected for subsequent installations:

▶ An incorrect SPDD modification adjustment led to a table conversion that lasted several hours.

▶ The number of parallel processes was set too low.

These experiences and tool runtimes were included in the schedule, and additional workdays were scheduled for the transition of the development systems. The exact scope of the adjustment activities could be determined using the sandbox systems and is within the previously estimated window. Figure 3.12 illustrates the milestone planning of the project.

Month	May				June					July				August			
Calendar Week	18	19	20	21	22	23	24	25	26	27	28	29	30	31	32	33	34
Project Activities																	
Requirements Phase																	
Project Kick-Off				■													
Evaluation of New Functions				■													
Selection of Required Business Functions				■													
Design Phase																	
Detailed Project Planning				■	■												
Creation of the Sandbox Landscape				■													
Update of SAP Solution Manager				■													
Identification of Technical Usages				■													
Planning of Technical Installation				■													
Creation of the Sandbox Landscape				■													
Download EHP4 & Stack XML				■													
EHP4 Test Installation in SAP NetWeaver ERP Sandbox				■													
EHP4 Test Installation in SAP NetWeaver Portal Sandbox				■													
EHP4 Test Installation in SAP NetWeaver BW Sandbox				■													
Build & Test Phase																	
System Copies of the DEV Landscape					■	■											
Start of Double Maintenance					■												
EHP4/EHP1 Installation in DEV Landscape						■	■										
Adjustments of Modifications (Transaction SPDD)							■										
Adjustments of Modifications (Transaction SPAU)								■									
Technical Tests and Corrections								■									
EHP4/EHP1 Installation in QAS Landscape									■								
Transport of Corrections and Adjustments									■	■							
Test of Core Processes incl. Interfaces										■	■						
Test Evaluations and Final Corrections											■	■					
Final "Go" Decision for Production												■					
Deploy Phase																	
Technical Preparation (Building Up the Shadow System)													■				
Go-Live (Saturday/Sunday)														■			
Support and Project Completion															■		

Figure 3.12 Milestone Planning of the Project

Phase 3: Build & Test

The transition of the development systems (DEV) and QAS went smoothly to a large extent, and the technical downtime was reduced by several hours due to the defined measures. To reduce the duration of the manual postprocessing work at the transition weekend, the SPAU transport to the enhancement package installation in the QAS system of the SAP ERP 6.0 landscape was integrated, in addition to the SPDD transport.

According to the installation cookbook, the Basis team provides the necessary input for creating the detailed cutover planning. Two weeks in the *Build & Test* phase are scheduled for test activities (regression test). Thanks to the additional user department support, critical errors could be solved by the end of the test cycle. After the evaluation of the test results, the official "go" is provided for the production transition as planned.

Phase 4: Deploy

The Basis team decided to begin with the technical preparations (for example, building up the shadow system) on the SAP ERP 6.0 production system (SAP ECC) one week before the transition weekend. This decision was based on the following reasoning:

▶ Less impact on the production due to the time expansion of the uptime phase

▶ Additional buffer time for error corrections

▶ Minimization of the risk of a delayed start of the technical downtime

This decision influenced the blocking time of the transport environment, which was now at the beginning of week 29. During the business downtime, fixed dates were agreed on to hold status meetings with the project team members and discuss deviations in the schedule and, if required, problems that occurred. The go-live went according to plan.

3.5.4 Summary

The project could be completed within the planned time and did not exceed the planned budget:

▶ Project duration: 9 weeks

▶ Double maintenance: 7 weeks

▶ Code freeze: 4 weeks

▶ Business downtime: 28 hours

▶ External consulting days: 8 days

For future maintenance projects, the enterprise plans to expand the sandbox approach to test critical processes already at an early stage. After having utilized the full optimization potential, the technical downtime met the requirements and was reduced by several hours.

3.6 Eight Tips for a Successful Enhancement Package Project

This chapter concludes with an introduction of the eight most important tips for success for your enhancement package project:

► **Read the documentation, and take your time to carefully prepare the project.**
The first and most important rule is obvious and therefore rather trivial: Because enhancement packages introduce a lot of innovations, it is necessary to read the corresponding documentation. Reading this book is already a first step in the right direction.

► **Set up SAP Solution Manager early, and prepare it for operation.**
Update your SAP Solution Manager at an early stage (that is, before the enhancement package project starts), set it up, and familiarize yourself with creating a maintenance process in the Maintenance Optimizer.

► **Use the latest installation tools.**
At the beginning of the project, you should always use the latest versions of the tools. This way, you ensure the best possible maintenance level.

► **Actively plan the regular maintenance of your system landscape.**
Include SAP enhancement packages in your planning at an early stage to evaluate their functional added value. The basic requirement for this is a good coordination, particularly between the user department and IT. This is the only way you can ensure that the appropriate business functions and technical usages are selected and installed within the maintenance process.

► **Use a sandbox system for evaluation.**
If the user department needs a live system to select and evaluate the new functions, you should build up a sandbox system. Because business functions are not reversible, you should activate them in a sandbox system for testing purposes only.

► **Plan realistically.**
Schedule at least one week per system for each enhancement package installation with EHP Installer. For the first test installation on a sandbox system, you should plan even more generously.

► **Optimize the downtime.**
Early test runs let you better assess the exact runtime and downtime and optimize them, if necessary. You can find more information on this in Chapter 5, Section 5.3.6, Optimization Potential of Parallel Processes.

► **Plan the procedure for emergency corrections.**
Determine a strategy for providing the production system with emergency corrections during an enhancement package project. For more details, refer to Section 3.1.4. Change Management — Sandbox System and Double Maintenance.

Having the right tools is the foundation for working successfully. This chapter describes the central tools of an enhancement package implementation and how to best use them.

4   Implementation Tools and Service Offers

With enhancement packages, SAP has created a new delivery model that lets customers flexibly implement new functions with little effort. The technical provisioning of SAP enhancement packages is divided into two steps: First, you select and download the enhancement package subcomponents via the Maintenance Optimizer; second, you complete the technical installation of these packages in the SAP ERP system.

This chapter first explains the role of SAP Solution Manager in the installation process. In a step-by-step description, you'll learn which settings are required and how to download enhancement packages via a maintenance process. Then we'll look at the new installation tool, SAP EHP Installer. In addition to the structure of the tool, you'll also learn about the technical installation process and get a detailed description of the installation phases. Finally, this chapter provides you with an overview of the additional utilities and service offers that support you in installing enhancement packages.

4.1   SAP Solution Manager in Enhancement Package Implementation Projects

SAP Solution Manager is an integrative platform that centrally supports the lifecycle of a business solution — from conceptual design, to configuration, to live operation. For project leads, end users, and administrators, it provides central access to tools, methods, and preconfigured content, which you can use for the evaluation, implementation, and live operation of your system landscape.

The concept of *work centers*, which is available as of SAP Solution Manager 7.0 SP15, helps you manage your system landscape with a uniform navigation and quick access to information, both of which facilitate your daily work. Figure 4.1

shows an overview of the work centers of SAP Solution Manager, embedded into the Application Lifecycle Management methodology.

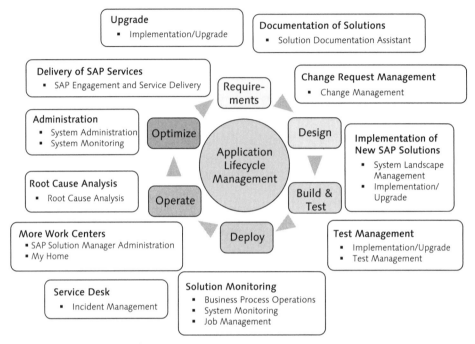

Figure 4.1 Work Centers of SAP Solution Manager

4.1.1 SAP Solution Manager Work Centers

The work center in SAP Solution Manager provides a central access point for managing and administrating your SAP solutions. The work centers are based on *Web Dynpro* technology and, compared to previous user interfaces, provide central and role-based access to the various work areas.

Each role grants access to a particular work center, which you can assign to a user depending on the range of tasks. Among others, the following work centers are available in SAP Solution Manager:

▶ System Landscape Management

▶ Change Management

▶ System Monitoring

▶ Test Management

Figure 4.1 provides a complete list of work centers. You start a work center in SAP Solution Manager using Transaction SOLMAN_WORKCENTER. This work center is divided into three navigation levels:

- The *navigation bar*, which lets you access the work centers via tabs
- A context-related *navigation area*, which grants access to views, typical tasks, and links within a work center
- The *content area*, which displays task-specific information and functions, depending on the view selected

Figure 4.2 shows the initial screen of the SYSTEM LANDSCAPE MANAGEMENT work center with the corresponding navigation levels.

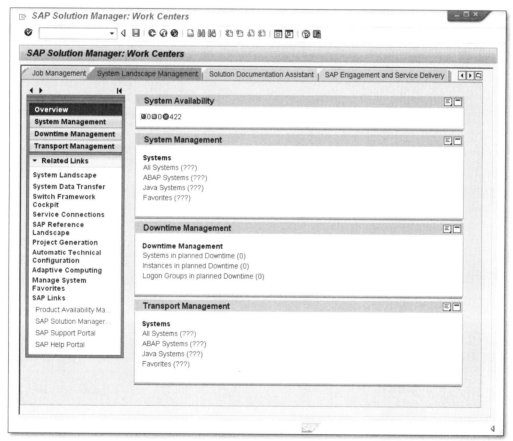

Figure 4.2 System Landscape Management Work Center

When implementing an enhancement package, you use the SYSTEM LANDSCAPE MANAGEMENT and CHANGE MANAGEMENT work centers. Sections 4.2, System Landscape in SAP Solution Manager, and 4.3, Maintenance Optimizer in SAP Solution Manager, examine the use of these work centers and guide you through the navigation with step-by-step instructions.

4.1.2 Prerequisites and Recommendations

This section introduces the prerequisites and recommendations that are relevant to enhancement package implementation projects:

▶ The use of SAP Solution Manager is a prerequisite for implementing an enhancement package implementation.

▶ Install the latest support package stack for SAP Solution Manager prior to implementing the enhancement package.

▶ Use the CHANGE MANAGEMENT and SYSTEM LANDSCAPE MANAGEMENT work centers in SAP Solution Manager, which you can start via Transaction SOLMAN_WORKCENTER.

▶ If necessary, define new SAP systems and system components using the System Landscape Directory (SLD).

▶ Start the technical preparations in SAP Solution Manager at an early stage.

4.1.3 Key Terminology

In addition to technical and project-organizational challenges, an enhancement package implementation project also has specific terminology. This section describes a selection of critical terms that are frequently used on the following pages.

▶ **Software product**
A product is a unit delivered by SAP and visible to the customer. A product is characterized by the following properties:

   ▶ It consists of smaller modules.

   ▶ In general, its overall purpose is to solve business tasks.

Examples of products are SAP ERP and SAP NetWeaver.

► **Software product version**

A product version is a particular release of a product whose components can be installed. Each product version has a clearly defined maintenance period.

There are complete product versions (for example, SAP ERP 6.0) and add-on product versions, which require existing product versions for installation (for example, enhancement package 4 for SAP ERP 6.0).

► **Product instance**

A product instance (or main instance) is part of a product version and is made up of several technically dependent software component versions. Product instances constitute the smallest installable unit that is installed and operated with a separate System ID (SID).

Examples of product instances include the SAP ECC Server, SAP NetWeaver Portal, SAP Self-Services (XSS), and SAP NetWeaver Business Warehouse (BW).

► **Technical usage**

A technical usage is a logical grouping unit that comprises interdependent product instances. In SAP enhancement packages for ERP, business functions are mapped to technical usages. They consist of one or more (ABAP-based or Java-based) product instances. Technical usages can only be installed on *existing* product instances.

Examples of technical usages are Central Applications, Human Capital Management, Financial Services, and Retail.

► **Software component**

A software component is a set of software objects that can be delivered together. Usually, there are multiple versions of software components. The individual software components are provided separately with support packages. Chapter 2, Section 2.2.2, Software Components of Enhancement Package 4 for SAP ERP, gives an overview of all of the software components that are delivered with enhancement package 4.

Examples of software components include SAP_BASIS, SAP_APPL, SAP-HR, EA-APPL, and EA-RETAIL.

► **Software component version**

A software component version is a unique version of a software component. Software component versions are part of a product instance, which, in turn, is part of a product version. A software component version is the smallest unit that can be delivered and maintained by SAP. Examples of software component versions are SAP_BASIS 700, SAP_APPL 600, SAP_APPL 604, SAP-HR 604, and EA-RETAIL 600.

▶ **SAP EHP Installer**
SAP EHP Installer is the installation tool for enhancement packages. In SAP documentations, it is sometimes referred to as *EHPi* or *SAPehpi*. You can download the tool from the SAP Service Marketplace at *http://service.sap.com/swdc* • DOWNLOAD • ENTRY BY APPLICATION GROUP • ADDITIONAL COMPONENTS • UPGRADE TOOLS • SAP EHP INSTALLER.

4.1.4 Overview of the Technical Activities

This section provides an overview of the technical activities for installing an enhancement package. They are described in detail in the following sections.

1. **Preparations in SAP Solution Manager**
   This refers to the settings in the SYSTEM LANDSCAPE MANAGEMENT work center. It includes, for example, integrating new SAP systems and creating a new logical component. For more information, see Section 4.2, System Landscape in SAP Solution Manager.

2. **Selection of the packages and creation of the package configuration file**
   This refers to the settings in the CHANGE MANAGEMENT work center. This includes, for example, creating a new maintenance process in the Maintenance Optimizer and downloading the packages. For more information, see Section 4.3, Maintenance Optimizer in SAP Solution Manager.

3. **Installation of the enhancement package**
   This is the tool-based installation process of the enhancement package in the SAP system landscape. For more information, see Sections 4.4, SAP Add-On Installation Tool, and 4.5, SAP EHP Installer.

Figure 4.3 illustrates the overall process of an enhancement package installation from the technical preparations and settings in SAP Solution Manager to the technical installation.

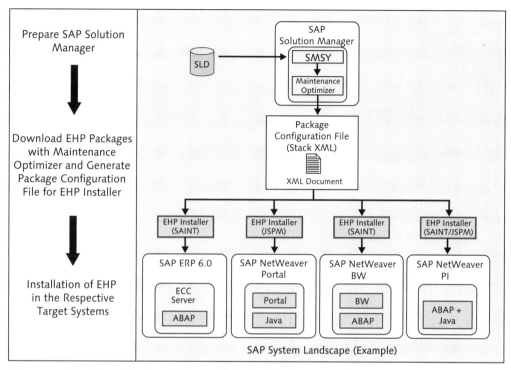

Figure 4.3 Overview of the Overall Process of the Technical Activities of an Enhancement Package Installation

4.2 System Landscape in SAP Solution Manager

Maintaining your SAP system landscape lays the foundation for creating maintenance processes in the Maintenance Optimizer. The system landscape in SAP Solution Manager can be considered a mapping of your actual system landscape. In general, there are two ways to access the system landscape in SAP Solution Manager:

▶ Via Transaction SMSY

▶ Via Transaction SOLMAN_WORKCENTER

The system landscape is part of the SYSTEM LANDSCAPE MANAGEMENT work center and the central access point for all business functions that are required to define and manage your system landscape. See Figure 4.2.

The following sections give you an overview of the settings that are required in SAP Solution Manager for installing an enhancement package for SAP ERP systems. If your system landscape is already maintained, you can perform the following steps to check your existing system configuration.

> **Note**
>
> You can find detailed instructions on the definition of systems in the SAP Help Portal at *http://help.sap.com* • SAP SOLUTION MANAGER <CURRENT RELEASE> • BASIC SETTINGS • SOLUTION MANAGER SYSTEM LANDSCAPE • CREATE SYSTEMS.

4.2.1 Automatic Creation of Systems Using the SLD

It is recommended that you define all systems and system components using the *System Landscape Directory* (SLD. If your SAP ERP landscape contains Java-based systems or dual-stack systems, the data transfer from the SLD is mandatory for automatically transferring the Java software component statuses. You can only create the system entries in the system landscape manually for pure ABAP-stack systems. Section 4.2.2, Manually Creating Systems in the System Landscape, provides more information on this.

Before you can replicate the system entries of the system landscape from the SLD, you must make sure that all relevant systems on the ABAP and Java side are registered in SLD.

Registering ABAP-Based Systems

To register an ABAP-based system in the SLD for the first time, proceed as follows:

1. Call Transaction RZ70 in the target system.

2. Enter the following information in the SLD BRIDGE: GATEWAY INFORMATION area:

   ▶ HOST: name of the host where the SLD is running

   ▶ SERVICE: port number on which the SLD is running

3. Click the DEFAULT button in the DATA COLLECTION PROGRAMS area, and confirm the dialog with YES.

4. Click the ACTIVATE CURRENT CONFIGURATION button.

5. Click the START DATA COLLECTOR AND JOB SCHEDULING button.

6. Now, log on to the SLD, and have the system display the technical systems that are registered in the SLD. Check to see if the system ID of your system is in the list of the ABAP-stack systems.

Registering Java-Based Systems

To register a Java-based system in the SLD, proceed as follows:

1. Start the Visual Administrator, and navigate to the HTTP SETTINGS node via the CLUSTER • SERVER • SERVICES • SLD DATA SUPPLIER • RUNTIME menu path.

2. Enter the following information in the HTTP CONNECTION area:
   ▶ HOST: name of the host where the SLD is running
   ▶ SERVICE: port number on which the SLD is running
   ▶ USER/PASSWORD: name and password of a user on the SLD host who has the *DataSupplierLD* role

3. Save your changes.

4. Click the TRIGGER DATA TRANSFER TO SYSTEM LANDSCAPE DIRECTORY (SLD) button to test the connection to the SLD.

5. If necessary, restart the SLD Data Supplier to force an immediate data transfer.

6. Log on to the SLD, and have the system display the technical systems that are registered in the SLD. Check to see if the system ID of your system is specified in the list of the Java-stack systems.

Registering Dual-Stack Systems

To register a dual-stack system in the SLD, you first need to register the ABAP part of the system. This procedure is identical to the procedure for pure ABAP-stack systems. Afterward, you have to separately register the Java part of the system in the SLD. This procedure is also identical to the procedure for pure Java-stack systems.

Automatically Transferring the Host Data

After registering your systems in the SLD, log on to your SAP Solution Manager. Check Transaction SM37 to see if the `LANDSCAPE_FETCH` background job is already scheduled. If the job doesn't exist yet, you can schedule it as follows:

1. Start the work center using Transaction SOLMAN_WORKCENTER, and navigate to the SYSTEM LANDSCAPE MANAGEMENT work center.

2. From the navigation area under RELATED LINKS, select the SYSTEM DATA TRANSFER ENTRY. This takes you to the SET UP SYSTEM LANDSCAPES • SAP SOLUTION MANAGER area via a new dialog box.

3. In the SYSTEM LANDSCAPE menu, select the SCHEDULE DATA TRANSFER FROM TMS/SLD entry.

4. Confirm the scheduling of the data transfer in the INITIAL DATA TRANSFER IN BATCH dialog box by clicking the YES button.

Alternatively, you can also schedule the data transfer using Transaction SMSY_SETUP. Please note that you still need to manually maintain some settings in the system landscape after the automatic transfer of the host data and system entries from the SLD. For more information, see Section 4.2.3, Necessary Manual Postprocessing.

4.2.2   Manually Creating Systems in the System Landscape

To create new systems and servers, start the work center via Transaction SOLMAN_WORKCENTER.

1. In the navigation bar, go to the SYSTEM LANDSCAPE MANAGEMENT tab.

2. From the navigation area under RELATED LINKS, select the SYSTEM LANDSCAPE entry (see Figure 4.2).

Alternatively, you can also access the system landscape via Transaction SMSY. If your system landscape has already been created, you can perform the following steps to check to see if your system data is fully maintained. Figure 4.4 displays the initial screen of the system landscape in SAP Solution Manager.

Manually Creating Host Data (Server)

Let's start by creating the host data. To do this, create the servers of the SAP systems you want to generate a maintenance process for.

1. In the SYSTEM LANDSCAPE initial screen, select the SERVER landscape component.

2. In the context menu (right-click on the SERVER landscape component), select the CREATE NEW SERVER entry.

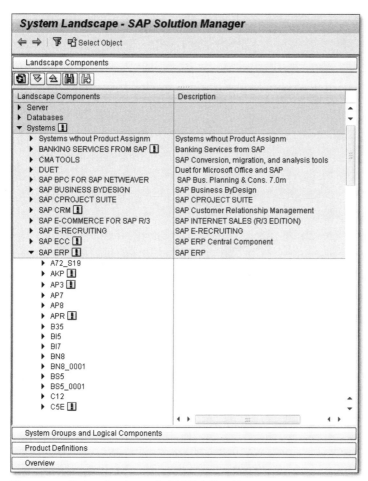

Figure 4.4 System Landscape in SAP Solution Manager

3. Enter the host name and save your entries.

4. Select the host name under the SERVER landscape component. On the right-hand side of the screen, you can maintain the details on the server. Enter your specifications in the various tabs — for example, the fully qualified host name in TECHNICAL DATA — and save your entries.

Manually Creating System Entries

Once you've created the servers of your landscape, you can proceed with the next step; that is, you can create the SAP system. Maintain all SAP systems of your product landscape for which you want to create a maintenance process.

1. In the initial screen of the system landscape, select the SYSTEMS component.

2. In the context menu (right-click on the SYSTEMS entry), select the CREATE NEW SYSTEM WITH WIZARD option.

3. Enter the system ID and all required data. Select a product and a product version from the input help. The correct product description for an SAP ERP 6.0 system (SAP ECC Server) is SAP ERP, the correct product version is SAP ERP 6.0. These specifications are also correct if you've already installed an enhancement package version in your SAP ERP system. Confirm your entries with NEXT.

4. Select the relevant main instances; for example, SAP ECC Server for an SAP ERP 6.0 system (SAP ECC Server). Bear in mind that only one ABAP instance per system can be defined as relevant. You can select additional ABAP instances in the ALSO INSTALLED column. Confirm your entries with NEXT.

5. Enter the system ID and the message server of your SAP system. Confirm your entries with NEXT.

6. Choose the GENERATE RFC DESTINATION and ASSIGN RFC DESTINATION fields. Confirm your entries with NEXT, and exit the wizard by selecting COMPLETE.

4.2.3 Necessary Manual Postprocessing

After you've created a new system with the help of the system wizard or the SLD, manual postprocessing is required. Select the system ID of the newly created SAP ERP system, and navigate through the following tabs.

1. In the SELECTION OF MAIN INSTANCES tab, you need to define additional main instances as relevant if they are connected to your SAP ERP system. An ABAP-stack system is defined as relevant through the SAP ECC Server main instance.

2. If a Java product instance runs on another technical system (for example, on SAP NetWeaver Portal), select the SYSTEM COMPONENT checkbox, and enter the corresponding system ID as a Java system component, as shown in Figure 4.5.

3. If additional ABAP product instances are installed on your SAP system, select the corresponding entries in the ALSO INSTALLED IN RELEVANT ABAP MAIN INSTANCE field.

4. Enter any additional information on your system in the other tabs.

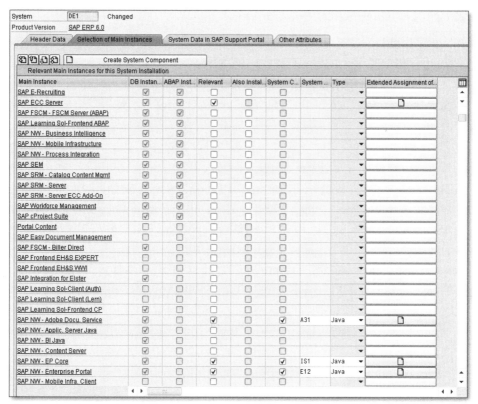

Figure 4.5 Selecting the Main Instances of an SAP ERP 6.0 System (SAP ECC Server) with Three Assigned Java System Components

---

Important Information

Check to see if the system data in the SOFTWARE COMPONENTS is up to date. If needed, update the system data using the READ SYSTEM DATA REMOTE button before you create a new maintenance process in the Maintenance Optimizer of your system. If required, reading the system data updates the version of the software component and the support packages that are entered in the SOFTWARE COMPONENTS tab.

The Maintenance Optimizer accesses the data of the system landscape in a new maintenance process and determines the required support packages based on the versions entered here.

4.2.4 Creating Logical Components

A logical component is an administrative entity that assigns logical systems in the system landscape and across projects to the following:

▶ A main instance of a product with a product version; for example, the SAP ECC Server main instance of the SAP ERP product with the SAP ERP 6.0 product version

▶ The various system roles within a project, for example, the *development system* role for the configuration

Logical components are always created for a product, such as SAP ERP, and should comprise all systems of a line (development, quality assurance, and production systems). The logical component of a product lets you create a maintenance process for the assigned systems.

You can also create a logical component in the system landscape of SAP Solution Manager. If you haven't created a logical component for the SAP ERP product yet, proceed as follows:

1. Navigate to the SYSTEM GROUPS AND LOGICAL COMPONENTS area in the system landscape.

2. Select the LOGICAL COMPONENTS menu area.

3. In the context menu (accessed by right-clicking on the LOGICAL COMPONENTS entry), select CREATE NEW LOGICAL COMPONENT. Ensure that the logical component is assigned to the SAP ERP product and the SAP ERP 6.0 product version. Confirm your entries.

4. The system displays detailed information on the logical component in the right-hand area of the screen. In the CURRENT SYSTEM ASSIGNMENTS tab, you maintain the various system types (for example, development, quality assurance, and production systems) of your SAP ERP product landscape.

5. Save your entries.

4.2.5 Summary

Let's summarize the individual steps again:

▶ Your SAP ERP systems are assigned to the SAP ERP product and the SAP ERP 6.0 product version in the system landscape.

▸ You've defined the relevant instances for each system to be maintained in the SELECTION OF MAIN INSTANCES tab in the system landscape. At least the SAP ECC Server main instance is defined as relevant.

▸ Additional system components of your landscape are defined as relevant in SELECTION OF MAIN INSTANCES, and the information on the system type (for example, Java) is maintained.

▸ The software component versions and the support package versions of your systems are up to date.

▸ A new logical component was created, if required, and the SAP ERP systems of your system line are contained therein.

This concludes the required settings in the system landscape of the SYSTEM LANDSCAPE MANAGEMENT work center. Section 4.3 presents the Maintenance Optimizer, which is part of the CHANGE MANAGEMENT work center, and describes how to create a new maintenance process to download enhancement packages.

4.3   Maintenance Optimizer in SAP Solution Manager

Solution maintenance has become considerably more complex and time-consuming over the years. In an SAP ERP system, for example, the number of software components has increased considerably. Chapter 2, Section 2.1, Brief Introduction to the Development of the SAP ERP Architecture, provides more information on this topic. In SAP R/3 4.6C, a system consisted of approximately five different software components; today — with SAP ERP 6.0 (the SAP ECC Server) — there are more than fifty components. Each software component has its own support packages, which SAP provides bundled as support package stacks. To make things easy, SAP provides a tool that clearly shows the maintenance processes in a clear format and supports you in the planning and implementation of maintenance activities: the Maintenance Optimizer. In general, there are two ways you can access the Maintenance Optimizer in SAP Solution Manager:

▸ **Via Transaction SOLUTION_MANAGER**
Select a solution in the SOLUTION OVERVIEW. In the CHANGE MANAGEMENT tab go to the MAINTENANCE OPTIMIZER entry. Click the CREATE NEW MAINTENANCE TRANSACTION button.

You can find a detailed description on downloading enhancement packages using Transaction SOLUTION_MANAGER in the document "How to Install EHP4: A Practical Guide" (at *http://service. sap.com/erp-inst* • SAP ENHANCE-

MENT PACKAGES FOR SAP ERP 6.0 • SAP ENHANCEMENT PACKAGE 4 FOR SAP ERP 6.0).

► **Via Transaction SOLMAN_WORKCENTER**
Section 4.3.2, Downloading an Enhancement Package for SAP ERP, provides a step-by-step description on how to create a new maintenance transaction via this transaction. This procedure is recommended by SAP.

Figure 4.6 shows the CHANGE MANAGEMENT work center of SAP Solution Manager. In the OVERVIEW area, you can get an overview of all your maintenance activities in your system landscape. Moreover, from the CHANGE MANAGEMENT work center you can start the *guided procedure* of the Maintenance Optimizer, which guides you through the planning and download of support package stacks and enhancement packages, for example.

Note

Support package stacks contain specific combinations of several support packages and patches for a software product version. This bundling forms a consistent unit, taking into account the technical dependencies.

The *SP Stack Schedule*, which you can view in the SAP Service Marketplace at *http://service.sap.com/sp-stacks* • SP STACK SCHEDULE, provides information on delivery dates for support package stacks.

A special SAP Note is published for each support package stack. This note is a list of the support packages contained in the support package stack, and useful information and references. You can find these SAP notes at *http://service.sap.com/notes* using the search term "Release & Information Note" (RIN).

4.3.1 Basic Settings in the Maintenance Optimizer

Before you can use the Maintenance Optimizer, you need to make some basic settings for creating a maintenance transaction. The information page of the Maintenance Optimizer in the SAP Service Marketplace, which you can access via *http://service.sap.com/mopz*, is a good place to start. There you can find, for example, a description of the basic settings, an overview of frequently asked questions and their answers, and further information on the usage options of Maintenance Optimizer Another source of information is SAP Note 1024932, which provides a list of related SAP notes and documentation on this topic.

Figure 4.6 Initial Screen of the Change Management Work Center

4.3.2 Downloading an Enhancement Package for SAP ERP

This section describes how you can download enhancement packages for SAP ERP via a product maintenance transaction in the Maintenance Optimizer. The description is based on SAP Solution Manager 7.0 SP22.

1. Start Transaction SOLMAN_WORKCENTER, and navigate to the CHANGE MANAGEMENT work center (see Figure 4.6).

2. In the navigation area under COMMON TASKS, select the NEW MAINTENANCE TRANSACTION function.

The system opens a new window with the maintenance transaction that consists of various steps (see Figure 4.7).

> **Note**
>
> The Maintenance Optimizer retrieves its system data exclusively from the system landscape of SAP Solution Manager. During maintenance transactions, it takes into account all of the main instances of the product version assigned to the system to be maintained that are marked as relevant.

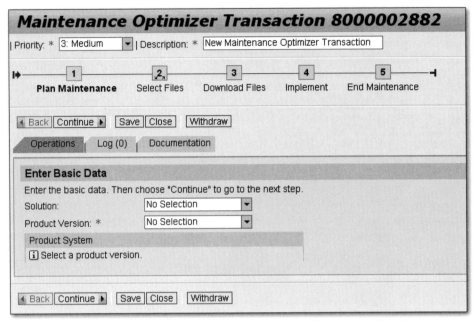

Figure 4.7 Initial Screen of the Maintenance Transaction of the Maintenance Optimizer

1. **Plan Maintenance**

   ▶ Enter the required information for this transaction; for example, a description of the maintenance transaction. Input is required for fields marked with a red asterisk.

   ▶ Optional: Select a solution from the value set.

   ▶ Select a product version, such as SAP ERP 6.0, for which you want to implement a maintenance transaction. The Maintenance Optimizer then suggests the systems that are created in the SAP ERP 6.0 product version in the system landscape.

   ▶ Select the systems where you want to install the enhancement package. In principle, you can create a maintenance transaction for one or more systems. For more information, refer to Chapter 5, Section 5.1.4, Special Features of the Package Configuration Files.

   ▶ Click the CONTINUE button to go to the next step.

2. **Select Files**

► Select the mode for receiving the files. Select CALCULATE FILES AUTOMATI-CALLY.

► Confirm your entries with CONTINUE.

► Select the maintenance option, ENHANCEMENT PACKAGE INSTALLATION Confirm your entries with CONTINUE.

The Maintenance Optimizer displays up to seven additional steps in which you can select files for download. The number of additional steps may vary depending on your entries in these additional steps.

1. **Additional step: Choose Stack**

► Select the enhancement package version you want to install After you've specified the enhancement package version, the system automatically suggests a support package stack in the next value set. Select the desired version of the target stack. Choose STACK DETAILS to view the support packages contained therein.

► You now see a list of the relevant technical usages. Activate the checkboxes of the technical usages you want to install. You can only select a technical usage if the prerequisites for the installation are met; that is, the required instance must be marked as relevant in the system landscape of SAP Solution Manager (see Section 4.2.3, Necessary Manual Postprocessing).

► Technical usages whose prerequisites are not met are indicated in gray. If you click on the name of a gray technical usage, the system opens a list with detailed information on the corresponding prerequisites; for example, the required instance. The red list entries indicate the prerequisites are not met.

► Click CONTINUE to confirm your selection.

2. **Additional step: Confirm Target**

► The Maintenance Optimizer takes you to a list of systems for which maintenance files were determined. Select the SID of a system to display the package list in a new dialog window, and check your selection.

► Click CONTINUE to confirm this step.

3. **Additional step: Select Add-On Products**

► The Maintenance Optimizer shows a list of installable add-on products. Click on the checkboxes of all add-on products you want to install.

► Click the CONTINUE button to go to the next step.

4. **Additional step: Select OS/DB-Dependent Files**

   ▸ The Maintenance Optimizer shows a list of operating systems and databases. Click on the checkboxes that you need to combine your operating system and database.

   ▸ Click CONTINUE to confirm your selection.

5. **Additional step: Select Stack-Independent Files**

   ▸ If your selection contains files that are not assigned to a stack, the Maintenance Optimizer now displays the files with no stack.

   ▸ Click the CONTINUE button to go to the next step.

6. **Additional step: Select Stack-Dependent Files**

   ▸ The Maintenance Optimizer shows a list of files that are part of a stack. Check this selection.

   ▸ Click CONTINUE to confirm your selection.

7. **Additional step: Confirm Selection**

   ▸ Select the tool you want to use to download the determined packages; for example, *download basket* or SLM.

   ▸ Click CONTINUE to confirm your selection.

8. **Download Files**

   ▸ When you select DOWNLOAD BASKET, the Maintenance Optimizer informs you that the files were sent to your download basket; a separate confirmation is not required. Click the DOWNLOAD FILES FROM DOWNLOAD BASKET button to start the download process.

   ▸ The Maintenance Optimizer informs you about the file names of the package configuration files and the storage location.

   ▸ Choose CONTINUE when you've completed the download process.

9. **Implement**

   ▸ In a list you can specify the implementation status of the systems for which you've created this maintenance transaction. Select the COMPLETED status if the installation was implemented successfully. Only when you've selected the COMPLETED status for all systems can you continue with the next step.

   ▸ The Maintenance Optimizer shows a list of the packages confirmed. Here, you can view detailed information such as package attributes and import conditions. You also have the option of viewing a package-dependent report on side effects (*side-effect report*).

▶ In the SMALL CAPS: STACK FILES tab you can save the package configuration file in a local target directory on your workstation.

▶ Click CONTINUE to confirm this step.

10. **End Maintenance**

▶ End the maintenance transaction after the successful implementation. To do this, click the COMPLETE TRANSACTION button. Changes to the maintenance transaction can no longer be made.

4.3.3 Package Configuration File

Based on your selection, the Maintenance Optimizer generates a package configuration file in XML format (*stack XML*). The package configuration file includes a list of all packages that are imported into your SAP system, as shown in the excerpt of Figure 4.8. The implementation tool (for example, EHP Installer) needs this file to execute the installation. Using the package configuration file, all selected packages are imported during the enhancement package installation. You can find the package configuration file in the *Electronic Parcel Service inbox* (EPS inbox) of SAP Solution Manager under /USR/SAP/TRANS/EPS/IN.

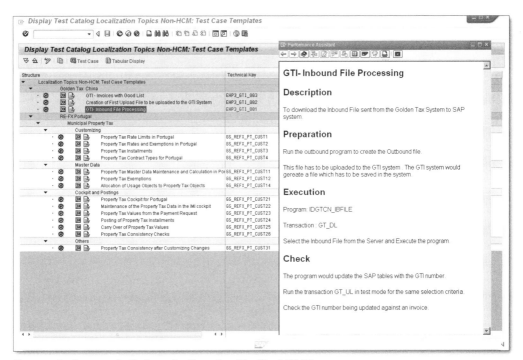

Figure 4.8 Excerpt of a Package Configuration File (Stack XML)

> **Practical Tip**
>
> In a dialog step of EHP Installer you must enter the path to your download directory. This directory can either be a local directory on your central instance or an integrated directory. Ensure that the following data is available in this download directory:
>
> ▶ All packages that the Maintenance Optimizer determined in the maintenance transaction
>
> ▶ Package configuration files
>
> ▶ Kernel archives
>
> ▶ Current versions of the tp and R3trans transport programs (as archives)

4.4 SAP Add-On Installation Tool

The SAP Add-On Installation Tool (SAINT) is the released import tool for older enhancement package versions for SAP ERP 6.0 systems (SAP ECC Server). Using Transaction SAINT, you can install enhancement packages up to and including enhancement package 3. With SAP enhancement package 4, the new installation tool, SAP EHP Installer, was launched. Only customers that operate the SAP ERP systems on a 32-bit architecture must import enhancement package 4 using SAINT. Currently, EHP Installer is not available for 32-bit platforms.

4.4.1 Differences to the EHP Installer

The installation process using the SAP Add-On Installation Tool (SAINT) differs fundamentally from an enhancement package installation using EHP Installer. The essential differences are as follows:

▶ The SAP Add-On Installation Tool is a pure ABAP-based installation tool and can be called via Transaction SAINT.

▶ The tool update is carried out via SAP Patch Manager (SPAM) update packages.

▶ Access to the operating system is not mandatory for the technical import process.

▶ Java components of an enhancement package are installed exclusively with the *Java Support Package Manager* (JSPM), up to and including enhancement package 3.

▸ The technical import conditions must be checked in the preparation phase based on SAP notes.

▸ An installation using SAINT is a resumable process that is similar to importing support packages.

▸ There is no separate instance (shadow instance) for downtime minimization.

▸ During the import process, the SAP ERP system should not be used in production, and you shouldn't import transports or run background jobs.

▸ The SAP ERP system is not restarted during the import process. A restart is required if you exchange the kernel archives together with the enhancement package installation (as of enhancement package 4).

▸ To optimize the import runtime, you are provided with the options PARALLEL IMPORT (SAP Note 1309506) and DOWNTIME MINIMIZED (SAP Notes 744343 and 1293666).

▸ With SAINT you can't implement enhancement package 4 in *one* installation step. You first need to import enhancement package 3; then you can install enhancement package 4. Make sure to take this into consideration when you plan the technical downtime for the production system.

4.4.2 "Downtime Minimized" Option

If you want to reduce the downtime for importing SAINT to a minimum, you can use the DOWNTIME MINIMIZED import mode. In this process, SAINT executes some of the phases in the live operation and prompts you during the import to end the live operation. You are also notified when you can start the live operation again.

The disadvantage of this procedure is that the system is changed by the imports during its use in production, so the point of no return and the start of the downtime do not coincide. The point of no return starts with the import module, *Import 1*. Resetting the installation is then only possible by importing a database backup. In this context, you must by refer to SAP Note 744343.

Moreover, you should note that the DOWNTIME MINIMIZED option in the SAINT cannot be compared to the downtime minimized approach of EHP Installer. EHP Installer forms a parallel instance (shadow instance) during the live operation in which all installations steps are executed. Therefore the EHP Installer does not work in the actual live instance until the technical downtime starts; e.g., when switching to the new repository takes place. This procedure, which is called a *system switch*, is described in detail in Section 4.5.3, The System Switch Procedure of

EHP Installer. For the sake of completeness, you should note that EHP Installer imports some transports into the production system before the technical downtime and generates new indexes, if required.

In the SAP Service Marketplace at *http://service.sap.com/erp-inst* • SAP ERP • SAP ERP 6.0 • SAP ENHANCEMENT PACKAGE FOR SAP ERP, you can find the installation guide for installing an enhancement package using SAINT. This guideline is called "Installation Guide SAP ERP 6.0 Enhancement Package 4 Using SAINT/JSPM."

4.5 SAP EHP Installer

This section covers the SAP EHP Installer installation tool, which was released with the implementation of enhancement package 4 for installations. EHP Installer is based on the upgrade tool *SAPup*, and uses the system switch procedure. In comparison to traditional installation tools like SAINT, this procedure enables a considerable reduction of the technical downtime and has been tested and optimized successfully in recent years (see Section 4.5.3, The System Switch Procedure of EHP Installer).

Besides the system switch procedure, EHP Installer also provides a newly designed graphical user interface. Along with this new design, all user dialogs were revised and made more user friendly. In addition, the majority of technical information is now directly read from the system; only customer-specific information must be entered via user dialogs. Furthermore, the error messages were considerably improved with more meaningful texts and with additional information and references to log files. Another optimization was achieved by standardizing the new user interface, *Software Delivery Tool* (SDT GUI), for the following system types:

▶ ABAP-stack systems

▶ Java-stack systems

▶ Dual-stack systems (ABAP and Java)

In the past, two different user interfaces were required for an enhancement package installation in these system types. In the case of dual-stack systems, these even had to be operated in parallel. With EHP Installer, you can edit these system types with a standardized user interface, which is a considerably more user friendly.

Now let's look at the installation tool, EHP Installer. The following sections use path specifications for Unix operating systems. For path specifications for other operating system types, refer to the installation document.

Note

EHP Installer has been enhanced once again in its functional scope: Besides the installation of enhancement packages, you can now also use it for *pure support package installations*. In maintenance projects without enhancement packages, only the *SAP Patch Manager* (SPAM) has been released so far. So now you can select between two tools for ABAP-stack systems:

- SPAM
- EHP Installer

EHP Installer is particularly suited for installing a larger number of support package stacks in a maintenance project. Using EHP Installer technology, you can considerably reduce the system downtime in comparison to the SPAM.

4.5.1 Key Terminology

The system switch procedure used today has a long development history. Before discussing the procedure in more detail, however, let's first outline some terminology for a better understanding:

- **Repository**
  The repository is the central storage for all development objects of the ABAP Workbench — for example, programs, table definitions, dynpros, function modules, or classes — and it is used across clients. The entire repository is in the form of client-independent tables at the database level. One of the main activities of an upgrade or enhancement package installation is to replace development objects in the repository with new versions that are delivered with the new release or enhancement package.

- **Shadow repository**
  In the system switch procedure, a temporary shadow repository is created in parallel to the repository of the source system. In this shadow repository, you can import new versions of the development objects while production work continues in the original system. At the database level, the shadow repository consists of *shadow tables*, whose names often only differ in the ending ~ from the name of the original table in most database platforms. However, some client-dependent shadow tables are created too. Although they are not part of the repository in the narrower sense, they are indispensable for operating the shadow instance.

- **Shadow instance**
  A shadow instance is a minimal ABAP system instance created in parallel to the

source system. Contrary to the original instance, the shadow instance only accesses the shadow repository. The combination of the shadow instance and the shadow repository forms the shadow system, which was used for the first time with the system switch upgrade technology.

▶ **Repository switch**
The repository switch procedure involves an upgrade technology that was developed for reducing downtime. The main purpose of this procedure is the creation of a shadow repository (formerly without a shadow instance) in parallel to the live operation and the switching of the repository to the technical downtime.

▶ **System switch**
The system switch procedure was introduced with SAP Web Application Server 6.10 and is still used today; it is a further development of the repository switch procedure. In addition to the shadow repository, a new SAP instance, the shadow instance, is generated that has access to the tables of the shadow repository. The shadow instance enables the manual adjustment of the data dictionary (DDIC) modifications and the activation of the objects in parallel to the live operation. The switch to the new repository takes place in the technical downtime. This advanced technology enables a significant reduction of system downtime.

4.5.2 Development from the Repository Switch to the System Switch Procedure

The *repository switch procedure* was established with the upgrade from SAP R/3 2.2 to SAP R/3 3.0. With this procedure, it was possible to considerably reduce the technical system downtime for the first time. Parallel to the live operation, a new repository was created in the background of the live repository, in which an early main import was executed. The switching to the new repository didn't take place until the technical downtime, though the manual adjustment of the data dictionary modifications, and long-running phases (for example, the activation of the DDIC), were still part of the technical downtime.

In the years following the release of SAP R/3 3.0, system downtime became more significance to enterprises, often due to increasing globalization. As a result, a new or improved procedure for reducing this downtime became the goal of SAP development. Different technologies were discussed and compared; finally, SAP decided to further develop the existing procedure, the *system switch upgrade,* which is still used successfully today. EHP Installer also uses the system switch upgrade procedure, but in an adjusted form. To illustrate this distinction, it is referred to as the *system switch procedure* in the SAP enhancement package installation.

4.5.3 The System Switch Procedure of EHP Installer

Now let's focus on the system switch procedure used by EHP Installer. Prior to the actual technical downtime, a comprehensive technical installation preparation and preprocessing takes place while the regular live operation continues. This period is referred to as *installation uptime* (or *uptime* for short).

One of the first steps during uptime is to generate a shadow instance. The required directory structure at the operating system level is created in the installation directory of EHP Installer under EHPI/ABAP/<SAPSID>. The shadow instance is prepared for the creation of the shadow repository later in the installation.

The actual shadow repository is generated in the DBCLONE phase. But unlike a technical upgrade, the shadow repository is not created from the export media of the new SAP release version, but from the original system. This process occurs in parallel to the live operation and is referred to as the *clone process* or *system clone*. To create the shadow repository, you copy the client-independent repository tables of the original system and selected client-dependent tables as shadow tables (see Figure 4.9). Because the term *clone* is often confused with a one-to-one copy of the original system, we want to emphasize once again that the only tables copied are those that are required for the operation of the shadow instance. Large tables with application data are not usually copied.

The creation of the shadow repository and various other activities in the shadow system can be implemented in parallel. If the number of parallel uptime processes (*maximum uptime processes*) is too high, this can compromise the live operation (see Chapter 5, Section 5.3, Analysis and Optimization of an Enhancement Package Installation). The shadow system is started for the first time in the START_SHDI_FIRST phase. During the uptime, the following steps, which characterize the system switch procedure, are performed in the shadow system:

▶ Modification adjustment of the data dictionary objects (Transaction SPDD).

▶ Activation of inactive DDIC objects in the ACT_UPG phase. The inactive dictionary objects can originate from both the enhancement packages and the relevant support packages or customer-specific transports.

▶ Distribution of activated DDIC objects in the PARDIST_SHD phase. In this phase it is decided whether and when the relevant database objects must be changed, and the necessary database statements are predefined.

▶ An early main import (SHADOW_IMPORT_* phases), which imports the majority of the new support packages, enhancement packages, and installed add-on packages (with kernel tools) into the shadow repository.

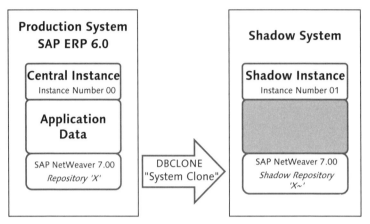

Figure 4.9 Creating the Shadow Repository (Schematic Display)

After these steps, the shadow repository is almost complete and contains a consistent description of the target system's table structure. However, it is still separated from the original system. The shadow instance is stopped and deleted before the technical downtime, or more precisely, in the STOP_SHDI_LAST phase. The shadow instance (caution: not the shadow repository!) is generated for one purpose: So that the administrator or developer can log on to the shadow system to implement the modification adjustment of the data dictionary objects, and then remove activation errors.

Switching to the new repository only occurs during the technical downtime and when importing the pending data. The repository switch works as follows: The repository tables of the original system are deleted (but not the tables including the application data!), and the corresponding tables of the shadow repository are renamed from X~ to X (x stands for the table name).

The switch to the new repository takes place in the first half of the technical downtime. The new SAP kernel is also exchanged, and the SAP instance profile is adjusted. All downstream activities run on the "new" instance. These include, for example, the main import, the import of outstanding transport requests, the implementation of tables with application data, the execution of programs, and other phases.

One side effect of this system switch procedure is that additional hardware resources are required for the shadow instance:

▸ Disk space (in the database instance)

▸ Processor performance (CPU)

▸ Memory; that is, available physical main memory

It is therefore also possible to install the shadow instance on a physically separate host; Chapter 5, Section 5.2.4, Configuring EHP Installer (Preconfigured Modes), provides detailed information on this topic. The shadow instance, however, is generated in a minimum configuration, and the required hardware resources are usually available in the hardware of the production system.

4.5.4 Supported Tools for the Enhancement Package Installation

The release of EHP Installer took place together with the implementation of enhancement package 4 for SAP ERP 6.0 and enhancement package 1 for SAP NetWeaver 7.0. Older enhancement package versions are installed using SAINT and JSPM. You can use Table 4.1 to determine the respective released tools for installing enhancement packages.

SAP Enhancement Package Versions	SAINT	JSPM	EHP Installer
Enhancement packages 2 and 3 for SAP ERP	✔	✔	✘
As of enhancement package 4 for SAP ERP	✘ *	✘ **	✔
Enhancement package 1 for SAP Solution Manager 7.0	✔	✔	✘
Enhancement package 1 for SAP NetWeaver PI 7.1	✘	✘	✔
Enhancement package 1 for SAP NetWeaver 7.0	✘	✘	✔

*Exception: EHP Installer is only released for 64-bit platforms. Enhancement package 4 installations on 32-bit platforms must be implemented using SAINT.

**Exception: JSPM can only be used if no enhancement package 1 for SAP NetWeaver is installed together with the enhancement package 4 installation (SAP NetWeaver systems only).

Table 4.1 Supported Tools for SAP Enhancement Packages

Refer to SAP Note 1256600 for installing enhancement packages. SAP Note 1245473 discusses current developments, changes, and important information on EHP Installer.

4.5.5 Technical Structure of the Installation Program

In the past, you had to use different user interfaces for ABAP-stack and Java-stack systems in case of an upgrade or an enhancement package installation. Both system types use separate programs that work with system-specific control programs (server programs). With EHP Installer, the different control programs have been harmonized. Although stack-individual installation programs are still used, such as the SAPehpi program for ABAP-stack systems and the SAPJup program for Java-stack systems, they are now capable of communicating with *one* control program, *Software Logistics Controller* (SL Controller), as shown in Figure 4.10.

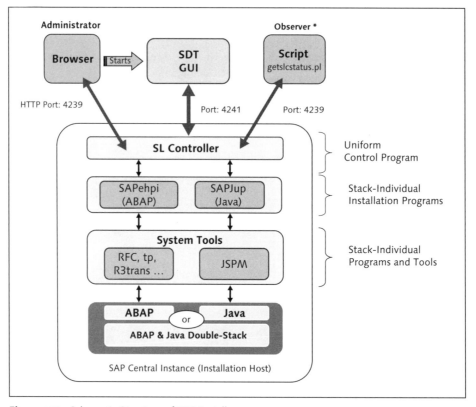

Figure 4.10 Schematic Structure of EHP Installer

Before discussing the design of the graphical user interface in more detail, let's first take a look at the structure of EHP Installer. EHP Installer is structured as a two-level client-server application. The individual parts of the application include the following:

► The front-end tool, Software Delivery Tool GUI (SDT GUI

► The server program, Software Logistics Controller

Front-End Tool SDT GUI

SDT GUI is the central user interface of EHP Installer. SDT GUI forwards all user entries and commands for starting, stopping, or repeating a phase to SL Controller.

SDT GUI manages the user role of the *administrator*. The administrator is authorized to make dialog entries, start and stop the installation, or repeat individual phases. The *observer* mode is only authorized to query the installation status. The observer mode is not currently included in the standard scope of EHP Installer.

Server Program SL Controller

SL Controller is the next step of the Upgrade Assistant Server (UA Server), and is used both for enhancement package installations with EHP Installer and in new upgrade tools. SL Controller can be used in multiple tools; that is, it can work with both ABAP and Java programs, as shown in Figure 4.10.

When EHP Installer is used, you don't start SL Controller directly, but via a script called STARTUP (Windows: STARTUP.BAT), which is executed in the SAP central instance and which starts SL Controller automatically. SL Controller requires an authentication of the user via a password. SL Controller itself, however, doesn't execute any technical changes to the SAP system. Its function can be described by the term *control module,* because its main tasks are to forward user input and control and monitor the communication between the user frontend and the installation process. Depending on the system type, SL Controller works with the SAPehpi program for ABAP-stack systems, or the SAPJup program for Java-stack systems. In the case of dual-stack systems, it communicates with the two programs in parallel. The SAPehpi and SAPJup programs implement the technical installation activities. In doing so, they access secondary programs; for example, JSMP or the tp transport control program, if required.

The task area of SL Controller can be illustrated based on a practical example: A user dialog prompts the administrator to enter the password of the DDIC user. After the administrator has entered the password via the user frontend, he confirms his entry with CONTINUE. SL Controller receives the entry confirmation and forwards it to the SAPehpi program, which then starts a *remote function call* (RFC) to the SAP system and checks the entered password for the DDIC user. If the password entered is incorrect, the RFC call cancels with an error code. This information, in turn, is forwarded to the SAPehpi program, which then creates a new user dialog with the additional message that the password entered was incorrect. It then transfers the dialog to SL Controller, which displays the new dialog window for the user via SDT GUI. In this new dialog window with the error message, the administrator can reenter the DDIC password. After the password has been entered again, the administrator can confirm his entry with CONTINUE. If the entry is correct, the installation continues.

4.5.6 Communication Routine

The SL Controller server program is started on the installation host, the SAP central instance; the user interface, STD GUI, however, can optionally be started on the workstation. The only communication between these two components is via the dialogs of SDT GUI on the workstation.

To create the communication routine, start the installation program in the SAP central instance using the STARTUP script. SL Controller starts and waits on port 4241 for a connection to SDT GUI in the standard setting. The administrator has two options for establishing the connection to SL Controller:

► Via a direct call of SDT GUI using the *Dual Stack Upgrade GUI* (DSUGUI) program

► Via an indirect call of SDT GUI using an HTTP request, for example, an Internet browser

Both variants are designed in such a way that they can be executed on a workstation. The advantage of this communication routine is obvious: Even if the administrator ends the frontend tool (whether intentionally or due to a technical problem; for example, a defective network connection), SL Controller and the programs continue on the SAP central instance. So the enhancement package installation is continued without an active frontend tool. You can log on to SL Controller again later by starting the frontend tool.

If you decide to call SDT GUI via an Internet browser, this call is via the *http://<host name of central instance>:<port>* address. Port 4239 is used in the standard setting. The administrator can start SDT GUI via the Internet browser and access the phase list of the installation. A manual change of all port numbers is possible when you start SL Controller. Chapter 5, Section 5.2.3, Parallel Enhancement Package Installations on a Physical Host, provides the exact instructions.

The individual user entries are done via the graphical frontend, SDT GUI, and forwarded to SL Controller. It receives the commands; however, it doesn't execute them itself but forwards them to SAPehpi or SAPJup.

The installation programs process the information received and are responsible for the installation activity. In doing so, they access secondary programs if required; these programs execute further installation instructions. These secondary programs include, for example:

▶ The `tp` transport control program that starts one or more transport steps

▶ The `R3trans` transport program; for example, for a data import

▶ An RFC call that can start background jobs and reports via function modules

On the Java side, the JSPM is used to deploying process of software packages. In dual-stack installations, the secondary programs work in parallel.

Another task of the SAPehpi or SAPJup programs is to monitor and evaluate the program execution, to interrupt or continue the installation, and to forward a message to SL Controller in case of an error.

The entire installation process of an enhancement package installation using EHP Installer includes 500 phases that are processed successively. Some phases are done within a few seconds (for example, changing a field content of a table or setting a flag); other phases have runtimes that last for hours; for example, importing entries into control tables or executing reports and programs.

4.5.7 Starting EHP Installer

This section outlines the start process of the installation tool. You need two files for this: The enhancement package installation tool as an SAR archive and the SAP cryptographic software tool (JCE Policy archive). You can find both archives in the SAP Service Marketplace at *http://service.sap.com/swdc*. In the first step, you, as the `<SID>adm` user, extract the SAR archive to your SAP central instance with the following command:

```
SAPCAR - xvf <download directory>/<path>/<archive>.SAR
```

This process creates the installation directory called EHPI with numerous subdirectories at the operating system level. The directory structure as a whole is simply referred to as *installation directory* (see Section 4.5.8, Installation Directory). The installation directory contains the STARTUP start script (Windows: STARTUP.BAT), which the <SID>adm operating system user can execute using the command

```
/EHPI/STARTUP jce_policy_zip=<path specification JCE Policy archive>
```

This command starts SL Controller. In the next step, the frontend tool, SDT GUI, must be started via an Internet browser with the URL *http://<host name>:4239*, or by directly executing the SDT GUI program using the command

```
EHPI/sdt/exe/DSUGUI
```

All other interactions occur via the graphical user interface. Refer to the technical documentation of EHP Installer in the SAP Service Marketplace at *http://service.sap.com/erp-inst* for further descriptions on the exact procedure of the start process.

4.5.8 Installation Directory

In the installation directory under /EHPI/ABAP/LOG you can find the log files on the installation, in addition to many installation-relevant files. This is also the storage location of the SAPEHPICONSOLE.LOG file, which documents the entire installation process. This file records user interactions with exact timestamps and exact start and end times for the installation phases. The SAPEHPICONSOLE.LOG file is a helpful utility for error and installation analysis. The /EHPI/ABAP/SAVE directory contains files that were saved during the enhancement package installation and can be reused for follow-up installations; for example, the instance profile of the shadow instance. The /EHPI/ABAP/TMP directory is the temporary directory of EHP Installer. Here, you can store, for example, transport files before and while the tp transport control program imports them. After the transport has been completed, they are moved to the /EHPI/ABAP/LOG directory. The /EHPI/ABAP/BIN and /EHPI/ABAP/MEM directories contain very sensitive files, such as the SAPehpi ABAP installation program, various library files, control files, and the "memory" of EHP Installer.

In the installation directory under the /EHPI/ABAP/EXE path, you can find the kernel programs that are used during the enhancement package installation. The directory of the shadow instance is stored under /EHPI/ABAP/<SID>. The /EHPI/SDT directory contains files for the frontend tool, SDT GUI. The /EHPI/JAVA structure comprises the executable files and log files of the Java components. Figure 4.11 shows the schematic structure of the installation directory.

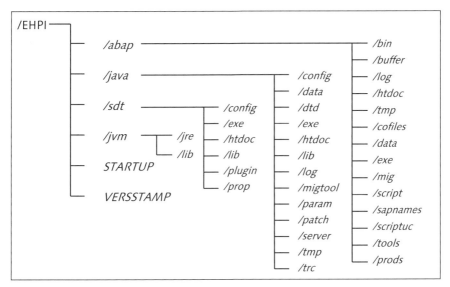

Figure 4.11 Structure of the Enhancement Package Installation Directory (First and Second Level)

4.5.9 Installation Interface SDT GUI

In the previous chapter, you learned that EHP Installer uses the user interface of Software Delivery Tool (SDT GUI). This newly designed graphical interface was introduced with SAP Business Suite 7 (Figure 4.12). Among other things, the new technology allows for the provision of a holistic frontend tool to ABAP-stack, Java-stack, and dual-stack systems.

SDT GUI lets you monitor the installation process and navigate through the individual installation steps (roadmap steps). The GUI consists of the following main elements:

- ▶ Menu bar
- ▶ Installation roadmap, including steps 1 through 8
- ▶ Tabs (for example, Monitor, ABAP, Java)
- ▶ Navigation buttons

The following sections present the SDT GUI functions individually (see Figure 4.12).

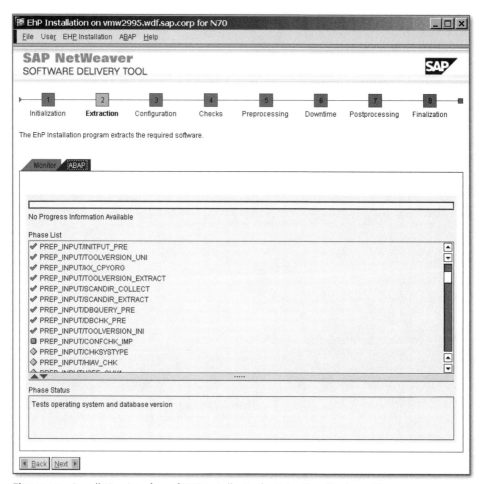

Figure 4.12 Installation Interface of EHP Installer in the Extraction Roadmap Step

Menu Bar

The menu bar offers various selection options for controlling an enhancement package installation. The most important menu options are the following:

▶ FILE

In this menu option you can close the user interface without terminating SL Controller. The installation process continues in the background.

▶ USER

In this menu option you can change the administrator password.

▶ ENHANCEMENT PACKAGE INSTALLATION
You are provided with selection options for immediate termination of the installation, and the option to completely reset the current installation with RESET INSTALLATION. This way, you undo all changes made by the installation. Your SAP system is then in the initial state it had prior to the installation. A reset of the installation in roadmap steps 1, 2, 3, or 4 is only possible using the BACK button.

▶ ABAP
The options in the ABAP menu entry are not required for regular installations. Use these options if the SAP support team requests you to do so.

▶ HELP
Various help offerings are available here.

Installation Roadmap

The installation phases are subdivided into eight consecutive steps, the *roadmap steps*, for example, roadmap step 1 (Initialization) or roadmap step 6 (Downtime). The active roadmap step is indicated in orange in the user interface. This highlighting helps you to monitor the progress of the installation. Section 4.5.10, Roadmap Steps of an Enhancement Package Installation, presents the individual installation steps in detail.

Tabs

The information and input area is subdivided into various tabs; for example, MONITOR and ABAP. The MONITOR tab informs you about the status of the respective roadmap step.

ABAP-stack systems have the ABAP tab; Java-stack systems, however, include the JAVA tab. Accordingly, both tabs are available for dual-stack systems. The required user entries during a roadmap step are made in the respective tabs of the stack. By switching between the tabs, you can conveniently handle enhancement package installations in dual-stack systems via a holistic frontend tool.

Navigation Buttons

Navigation between the roadmap steps is done using the control elements, BACK and NEXT, which supports an intuitive usage. If you are in roadmap steps 1 through 4, you can use the BACK button to completely reset the installation. Note, however, that you must manually delete the installation directory after a successful reset. The directories are created again by reextracting the SAR archive.

Practical Tip

Observer Mode and Alert Function

To activate the observer mode and the alert function, the following SAP Developer Network (SDN) blog provides useful tips:

https://www.sdn.sap.com/irj/scn/weblogs?blog=/pub/wlg/12870.

Both functions will be included again in the standard functional scope in a future version.

Scroll Mode

Officially, the scroll mode is no longer intended for installations. However, you can still start it for ABAP-only systems from the installation directory under /EHPI/ABAP/BIN using the command

```
SAPehpi gt=scroll
```

A tool that allows for session management at the shell level must be installed in the target system. The scroll mode does not provide you with any of the advanced features that are available in the user interface. Only use the scroll mode in exceptional cases.

4.5.10 Roadmap Steps of an Enhancement Package Installation

The eight consecutive roadmap steps describe the installation process from the start of the installation tool to the successful completion of the process. The installation consists of several hundred phases that are processed sequentially. These phases are grouped in eight logically consecutive roadmap steps (see Figure 4.13). Installation steps 1 through 4 prepare the system for the enhancement package installation. This is followed by the *Preprocessing* and *Downtime* steps. Subsequent to the technical downtime, various postprocessing tasks are performed for the installation, before you can close the user frontend in the last step (*Finalization*). The following pages present the individual roadmap steps to give you an impression of what happens in the background of the installation.

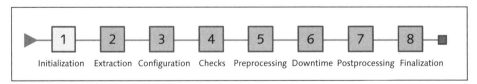

Figure 4.13 Roadmap Steps of EHP Installer

Roadmap Step 1: Initialization

In the *Initialization* roadmap step, SL Controller analyzes your system. To do this, the installed SAP system stacks are determined in the SAP central instance; for example, there are checks to see if your system is an ABAP-stack, Java-stack, or dual-stack system. According to this analysis, in the case of an ABAP-stack, for example, the ABAP tab is added to the user interface next to the MONITOR tab. The *Initialization* roadmap step is completed within a few seconds. When you click the NEXT button, the installation continues with the next roadmap step.

Roadmap Step 2: Extraction

In the *Extraction* roadmap step, the system settings are read and data is queried via the system. In the dialog windows, you must enter, for example, the enhancement package installation key, the path to your download directory, and the password of the DDIC user.

EHP Installer analyzes the content of the download directory and reads which enhancement package components and support packages are stored there. The packages are extracted in the SCANDIR_* phases and copied to the transport directory. The system kernel is copied to the installation directory under /EHPI/ABAP/ EXENEW and /EHPI/ABAP/EXE. The installation tool checks the DIR_PUT profile parameter and compares it with the path of the installation directory. If the values don't match, it automatically sets the DIR_PUT profile parameter to the value "EHPI/abap." As this roadmap step proceeds, ABAP tools, such as help reports, are imported into the system via transport.

The net runtime of the *Extraction* roadmap step amounts to a couple of minutes. To complete this phase, a dialog window appears including instructions and information on possible errors or warnings (see Figure 4.14). You can also find this information in the CHECKS.LOG file in the installation directory under /EHPI/ABAP/LOG (in case you should close the window accidentally). The history of the CHECKS. LOG file is included in the CHECKS.SAV file. Perform the necessary corrections, and repeat this phase. You can start the next roadmap step as soon as the dialog window no longer contains any error entries.

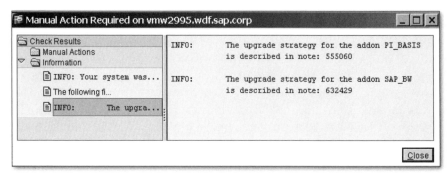

Figure 4.14 Dialog Window with Information and Instructions

Roadmap Step 3: Configuration

In the *Configuration* roadmap step, you must make some technical specifications on the installation. During your first installation, you should allow some extra time for this step. First, some configuration information on the installation is required.

Note

The preconfigured mode, MANUAL SELECTION OF PARAMETERS, is comparable with an expert mode. Select this option if you want to enter the detail information on the installation individually. You can use the expert mode, for example, to specify the number of batch, uptime, and R3trans processes individually, or to freely select the instance number of the shadow instance. For more information on preconfigured modes, refer to Section 5.2.4, Configuring EHP Installer (Preconfigured Modes).

During the EHP_INCLUSION phase, you will be asked to provide the package configuration file (stack XML). Enter the correct path to this stack XML file, which you've generated in SAP Solution Manager prior to the start of the installation. The stack XML file is stored in the /SAPMNT/TRANS/ EPS/IN directory of your Solution Manager (see Section 4.3.2, Downloading an Enhancement Package for SAP ERP, and Figure 4.8). If the stack XML file is stored in your download directory, the installation tool automatically offers it for selection. All support packages and enhancement package archives, which are located in the download directory, are then extracted to the <DIR_EPS_ROOT>/IN directory of the central instance (default: /SAPMNT/TRANS/EPS/IN). This may take some time. Subsequently, it is checked whether a valid installation queue can be created from the imported packages.

Later in the installation — more precisely, in the IS_SELECT phase — you obtain an overview of the add-ons installed in your system. Use the linked SAP notes to check which handling is suggested, and use this information to decide whether you can keep the add-on in its current version or whether you need to update it. Prior to the start of the installation, inquire about which strategy your add-on vendor supports. For more information on handling add-ons, refer to Chapter 5, Section 5.2.5, Handling Add-Ons in Enhancement Package Installations.

Caution: In the following phase, BIND_PATCH, you can add additional support packages to your installation queue; for example, the latest HR support packages or support packages for your add-on software. The installation tool checks to see if the equivalence of the support packages is met. (If warnings occur, do not ignore them under any circumstances! For more information on the topic of equivalence, refer to Chapter 2, Section 2.2.6, Support Package Strategy and Equivalence Levels.) The shadow instance is prepared over the course of this roadmap step and includes, for example, the generation of instance profiles.

Practical Tip

Check the parameters of the shadow instance profile. You can find the profile files in the installation directory under /EHPI/ABAP/<SID>/SYS/PROFILE. If sufficient hardware resources are available, you can add individual parameters or increase the buffer areas. This can positively influence the duration of the installation uptime.

At the end of this roadmap step, a new dialog window opens displaying information and instructions on errors and warnings. Repeat the roadmap step until all errors are removed.

Roadmap Step 4: Checks

The *Checks* roadmap step is the last step of the installation preparation. Until the end of this step, you have the option of resetting the installation using the BACK navigation button. In the subsequent installation step, *Preprocessing*, this is only possible via the RESET INSTALLATION menu option.

In this roadmap step, the installation tool examines whether the prerequisites required for the enhancement package installation are met. These prerequisites include, for example, whether the existing disk space meets the requirements of the installation. You are usually prompted to create new table spaces in the database and extend existing ones. Further examination steps check whether open or canceled updates exist in your system. These must be removed at the beginning of the *Downtime* roadmap step at the latest. The net runtime of the *Checks* roadmap step amounts to a couple of minutes. Note that the creation of new table spaces may take some time.

Roadmap Step 5: Preprocessing

At the beginning of the *Preprocessing* roadmap step — more precisely, in the REPACHK2 phase — you are prompted to lock the development environment. The result of locking the development environment in the development system is that transport requests can no longer be created, released, and transported. The development activities must cease with the confirmation of this lock (until the completion of the enhancement package installation).

The result of locking the development environment in a production system is that transports can no longer be carried out. Emergency corrections can only be implemented in the system directly. Consider here that possible corrections to the repository no longer exist in your production system after the system switch to the technical downtime. All manual changes to the repository have the potential to result in errors and cancelations of the installation routine. For this reason, carefully plan and communicate the setting of this lock in your enterprise.

The lock of the transport environment is followed by the creation of the shadow repository. In the DBCLONE installation phase (formerly RUN_RSDBSCPY), all required tables (caution: no application data!) of your production system are copied to the shadow database.

Practical Tip

You can monitor the progress of the DBCLONE phase using the DBCLONE<No.> background job in Transaction SM37, or directly at the operating system level using the log files DBCLONE<No.>.<SID>. To understand the creation of the shadow repository, you should take a look at the log file DBCLONE<No.>.<SID>, which is available in the /EHPI/ ABAP/TMP installation directory.

Example 1:

```
"START ENHTOOLS -> ENHTOOLS~"
"ENHTOOLS has 6 rows."
"ENHTOOLS DONE""1"
```

The ENHTOOLS table is copied ("cloned") and renamed to ENHTOOLS~. ENHTOOLS contains six entries that are transferred to the shadow repository.

Example 2:

```
"START ENHTOOLS_UVL -> ENHTOOLS_UVL~"
"ENHTOOLS_UVL content is not required."
"ENHTOOLS_UVL DONE""0"
```

The ENHTOOLS_UVL table is copied and renamed to ENHTOOLS_UVL~. The data content of the ENHTOOLS_UVL table is not required in the shadow repository.

The difference from the technical upgrade, which works with the SAPup program, is the way the shadow instance is created (see the Additional Information box). The SAPup program generates the shadow tables from the export media of the upgrade export DVDs, whereas EHP Installer creates the shadow tables from the basis tables of the original instance. A shadow system is only generated for an ABAP-stack system, not for a Java-stack system.

Additional Information
For a better understanding, you should know the following backgrounds: The following programs are used in a technical release change (upgrade):

- SAPup for an ABAP-stack system
- SAPJup for a Java-stack system
- SAPup and SAPJup for dual-stack systems

A shadow system (shadow instance and shadow repository) is only generated for the ABAP stack. The shadow repository is created from the export media of the upgrade export DVDs.

The following programs are used in an enhancement package installation using EHP Installer:

- SAPehpi for an ABAP-stack system
- SAPJup for a Java-stack system
- SAPehpi and SAPJup for dual-stack systems

A shadow system (shadow instance and shadow repository) is only generated for the ABAP stack. The shadow repository is created from the original system.

Over the course of this step, the data dictionary modifications in your system are determined. Execute the adjustment of the modifications from the shadow instance, and save the adjustment in *one* transport request. You can integrate this transport request with the enhancement package installation of your system line's subsequent systems without having to adjust the objects again manually. To do this, plan the corresponding transport request for export in Transaction SPDD. Don't confirm the successful adjustment of modifications until all objects are processed in Transaction SPDD; an incomplete adjustment can result in data loss. For more information on SPDD modification adjustment, refer to the installation guide of EHP Installer and the *Troubleshooting and Administration Guide* (see Chapter 5, Section 5.2.1, Additional Documentation and Information).

The successful adjustment of the object is followed by the ACT_UPG phase, which activates your customer objects and other SAP objects. An activation log provides information about the activation errors in this phase. It is absolutely necessary to carry out an in-depth analysis of the activation errors with subsequent manual removal. For more information, see Chapter 5, Section 5.2.7, Activation Errors in the ACT_UPG Phase.

The SHADOW_IMPORT_INC phase is the last time-consuming phase of the *Preprocessing* roadmap step. A large part of the objects of the integrated add-ons, support packages, and enhancement packages are now imported into the shadow repository. This step is also referred to as *shadow import* or *early main import*, which is significantly responsible for the reduction of the technical downtime. The shadow instance is already shut down at this point (STOP_SHDI_LAST phase), and can no longer be started; however, the shadow repository still exists. At the end of the *Preprocessing* roadmap step, in the DOWNCONF_TRANS phase, you are informed that your SAP system is now ready for technical downtime.

You are requested to stop the production activities in your system, lock the users, and (important!) save the installation directory (see Figure 4.15). In addition, save the instance profiles and the kernel directory of your SAP system. Once you've confirmed the dialog window, the SAP system is stopped, and you are requested to create a database backup. Make sure that you can recover the current system status using the data backup in case of technical problems; for example, hardware defects. Only after you've confirmed this dialog step does the next roadmap step, *Downtime*, begin.

> **Note**
>
> It is usually not necessary to create an offline backup of the database. Experience has shown that many customers usually use a *consistent* online backup (that is, including all archive logs). You can start an online backup in parallel to the live operation, which saves valuable time.

Experience has shown that the runtimes of the *Preprocessing* roadmap step are very specific in terms of hardware and installation. Without doubt, this step must not be underestimated with regard to the net runtime; it lasts several hours.

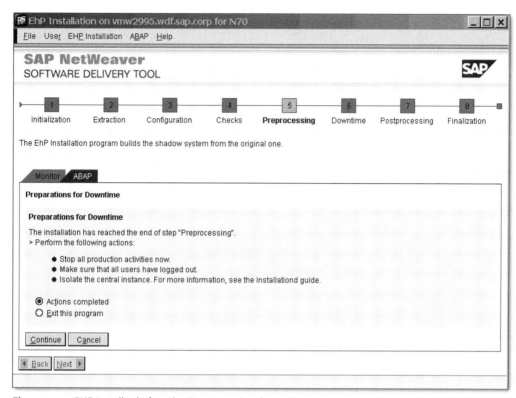

Figure 4.15 EHP Installer before the Downtime Roadmap Step

Roadmap Step 6: Downtime

The technical downtime is the core of an enhancement package installation. The SAP system cannot be accessed by an end user during this time, and it is stopped and started again several times (mainly for performance optimization). The *Downtime* roadmap step can be divided into two subareas:

1. Switching the tables and the kernel

2. Table conversion, main import, and program execution

Let's first consider the steps that are executed in part 1. The system is locked against logon at the beginning of the technical downtime; a logon is only possible with user DDIC in client 000, and the switching of the repository and the kernel is prepared. In the EU_SWITCH phase, the development environment is switched initially; that is, the original tables are deleted and the shadow tables that end with ~ are renamed to the original tables.

Let's consider the system switch technology more closely based on an example: In the DBCLONE phase (*Preprocessing* roadmap step), you created (i.e., cloned) the ENHTOOLS table with the same structure as the ENHTOOLS~ table. In the EU_SWITCH phase (*Downtime* roadmap step), the ENHTOOLS table is deleted in the original instance (drop table SQL command), and the ENHTOOLS~ shadow table is renamed to ENHTOOLS (rename table SQL command). The successful switching of the development environment is followed by the switching to the new kernel version. The new SAP kernel is copied from the /EHPI/ABAP/EXENEW installation directory to the kernel directory under /USR/SAP/<SID>/SYS/EXE/RUN of your original instance. This constitutes the end of the first downtime part.

Part 2 of the downtime is the actual main import. The following briefly outlines the most important phases:

▶ **PARCONV_UPG (parallel conversion)**
This phase comprises the parallel conversion; that is, the database tables are brought to the target status.

▶ **TABIM_UPG (table import)**
This phase comprises the table import; that is, the missing contents that could not be imported in the shadow import in the SHADOW_IMPORT_INC phase are now written to the target tables. The SAP system is shut down for the runtime optimization during the table import.

▶ **XPRAS_UPG (execute program after import of upgrade)**
Programs and after-import methods are executed in this phase.

If you've integrated an SPAU transport with adjusted repository objects into the installation, this transport is imported in the TABIM_UPG phase. One of the last activities of the *Downtime* roadmap step is the SAP system startup and unlocking the development environment, as you can see in the SAPehpiConsole.log log file:

```
>> <Date, time> START OF PHASE MAIN_NEWBAS/STARTSAP_PUPG
Unlocking SAP system ...
Unlocking development environment ...
Starting system ...
Restarting service ...
Starting system ...
System is available.
>> <Date, time>  END OF PHASE   MAIN_NEWBAS/STARTSAP_PUPG
```

You can find the SAPEHPICONSOLE.LOG log file in the installation directory under EHPI/ABAP/LOG. In your installation screen, the system displays the message that the downtime is over and the application servers can be started. The *Downtime* roadmap step ends when you confirm this dialog information. Section 5.3, Analysis and Optimization of an Enhancement Package Installation, provides information on the optimization of the technical downtime.

Roadmap Step 7: Postprocessing

In the *Postprocessing* roadmap step, the system informs you about some of the necessary manual technical postprocessing. This includes, among other things, scheduling background jobs, implementing a backup, and generating ABAP programs (SAP Load Generator, Transaction SGEN). The installation guide of EHP Installer, which you can find in the SAP Service Marketplace at *http://service.sap.com/erp-inst*, includes additional application-related and technical postprocessing.

> **Practical Tip**
>
> The dialogs in the *Postprocessing* installation step are for informational purposes only. It is usually not necessary to perform the described activities immediately. You can first complete the installation, end the installation tool, and implement the technical postprocessing all at once.

In the SPAUINFO phase, you obtain information about how many repository objects must be adjusted (Transaction SPAU).

Implement the modification adjustment in your SAP system, and save your adaptations in *one* transport request. End the adjustment in Transaction SPAU using the MARK REQUEST option. The transport number is then automatically written to the UMODAUTO.LST file and stored in the /SAPMNT/TRANS/BIN directory. For all subsequent enhancement package installations of your system line, you now have the option of integrating this SPAU transport request with the installation. Confirm the completed adjustment of modifications in the enhancement package installation tool, and continue with the installation.

Finally, a result report on your installation is created in the CREATE_UPGEVAL phase. This evaluation provides critical information about the runtimes of individual phases and forms the starting point of a detailed analysis for optimizing your installation. You can find the *UPGANA.XML* analysis file and the *UpgAnalysis. xsl* style sheet in your installation directory under /EHPI/ABAP/HTDOC. To view the analysis file in HTTP format, the style sheet must be located in the same directory at the operating system level. Section 5.3.3, Runtime Analysis File of an Enhancement Package Installation, provides more information on the content of the UPGANA.XML file.

The system prompts you to send the UPGANA.XML file to SAP. You should definitely use this option after each installation, because only with your runtime data can SAP ensure a permanent optimization of the installation tool. The installation concludes with the backup of the log files and the deletion of the installation directories that are no longer required. The pure runtime of the *Postprocessing* roadmap step amounts to a few minutes. When scheduling, though, you must take into account the implementation of the modification adjustment in Transaction SPAU in the installation of your development system. The duration for processing the modifications depends on their scope and the number of people involved in the adjustment.

Roadmap Step 8: Finalization

The *Finalization* roadmap step ends the installation tool and SL Controller in your SAP central instance. You can end the installation interface using the EXIT button. This installation step only takes a few seconds. Your enhancement package installation is now complete, and you can start with the technical postprocessing in accordance with the installation guide.

4.5.11 Installing Technical Usages Retroactively

You've installed SAP enhancement package 4 for SAP ERP using EHP Installer. After the installation, you realize that one or more technical usages have not been installed in this installation (for example, due to wrong selection in the maintenance transaction or because further functional requirements arose).

In this case, there is an exception rule for the usage of SAP Add-On Installation Tool (SAINT). The following conditions must be met to install additional technical usages in a 64-bit architecture using SAINT:

▶ All SAP NetWeaver software components must already correspond to Version 7.01; for example, SAP_Basis 701, SAP_ABA 701.

▶ A package configuration file (stack XML) that is generated by the Maintenance Optimizer is used.

▶ The package configuration file contains no new version of the SAP_APPL component.

Because of this, using SAINT is basically restricted to cases in which the *Central Applications* technical usage (or another technical usage that contains the SAP_ APPL 604 component) was installed using EHP Installer.

For the *initial* installation of enhancement package 4 on an SAP ERP 6.0 system (on a 64-bit operating system), you must use EHP Installer. Consider the additional work in your planning if you install individual technical usages retroactively (among others, in the installation, modification adjustment, and test effort areas).

4.5.12   Phase List for the Enhancement Package Installation

The phase list is a critical information source for installations using EHP Installer. It contains all of the installation phases and related information. Besides the full phase name and a brief description of the phase, it lists the name of the log and error files, as you can see in the excerpt of the phase list in Figure 4.16.

Module: *Import and Modification Transfer*					
Phase	**Arguments**	**Duration**	**UPGRADE Actions**	**Log Files**	**User Actions**
SQLDB_PARAMEU1	"PARAMEU1"		Performs actions for restart handling	PARAMEU1.LOG	
SETSYNC_DOWN_START_CLONE	"DOWNTIME" "STARTED"	dialog	events for sync with Jump		
SETSYNC_EULCK_START_CLONE	"EU_LOCKED" "STARTED"	dialog	events for sync with Jump		
ADJUSTCHK	"SAP_MOD_EHP" "ADJUSTCK.ELG" "ADJUSTMT.INF"		Determines ABAP Dictionary objects that need to be adjusted	ADJUSTCK.LOG	Confirm message, if necessary
DBCLONE_NODATA	"DBCND" "DBCLONE_NODATA.ELG" "NODATA"		Clones tables without data from original to the shadow system	DBCLONE_ND.LOG	
DBCLONE_DATA	"DBCWD" "DBCLONE_DATA.ELG" "DATA"		Clones tables with data from original to the shadow system	DBCLONE_WD.LOG	

Figure 4.16   Excerpt of the Phase List of an Enhancement Package Installation Using EHP Installer

You can find the PHASELIST.XML phase list and the SAPupPhaseList.XSL style sheet in your installation directory under /EHPI/ABAP/HTDOC. To open the phase list in HTML, the style sheet must be stored in the same directory.

Practical Tip

Use the phase list in the case of technical errors in the installation process as the first source to find out which activity is executed in the respective phase and which log files are written.

Example:

▶ Phase name: SCANDIR_PRP

▶ Action: *Scans the download directory and presets variables*

▶ Logs: *SCANDIRP.LOG*

▶ User action: No entry (that is, no user dialog in this phase)

From this list you can see that the download directory is read in the SCANDIR_PRP phase. The cause of a cancelation in this phase could be that the access authorizations for the download directory are not specified correctly.

4.6 Service Offers and Useful Utilities

SAP provides its customers with a variety of utilities and service offers for enhancement packages. This section is supposed to draw your attention to some offers that can support you in the planning and implementation of an enhancement package installation.

4.6.1 SAP Enhancement Package Info Center

SAP promised its customers to continuously provide new business processes; in this context, SAP has implemented an area in the SAP Service Marketplace that specifically provides information about SAP enhancement packages for SAP ERP. These pages serve as a central entry point for technical and functional information. The information ranges from the SAP enhancement strategy in general, to the overview of available enhancement package versions for SAP ERP 6.0 — including an overview of new functions, application areas, and benefits of business functions — to technical details. Besides a vast number of useful details, these pages also provide access to documentation, release information, and test catalogs. You can access the SAP Enhancement Package Info Center at *http://service.sap.com/erp-ehp*. The technical installation guides on EHP Installer are available in the SAP Service Marketplace at *http://service.sap.com/erp-inst*.

4.6.2 SAP Enhancement Package Experience Database

Evaluations on enhancement package projects in general, and specifications on project runtimes, downtimes, reasons for installing SAP enhancement packages, and so on are information customers often ask about. The *SAP Enhancement Package Experience Database,* also known as the *EHP Experience Database* (see Figure 4.17 and Chapter 3, Section 3.4, Enhancement Package Project Statistics) lets you access data and evaluations by SAP customers. The EHP Experience Database is available via the SAP Enhancement Package Info Center at *http://service.sap.com/erp-ehp* • SAP ENHANCEMENT PACKAGE EXPERIENCE DATABASE or at *http://service.sap.com/ehp-db*. An online questionnaire lets you give feedback on your experience. Your information is evaluated anonymously and incorporated in SAP's statistical database.

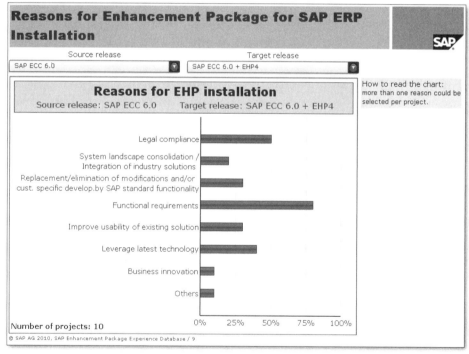

Figure 4.17 Excerpt of SAP Enhancement Experience Database

4.6.3 Solution Browser Tool

The *solution browser tool* is an application you can use to gather information on delta functions in a targeted manner. Start the solution browser tool via the URL *http://erp.fmpmedia.com* (see Figure 4.18). You can specify a language in the left area of the menu. Then select your current release version in the SOURCE RELEASE VERSION area (for example, *SAP ERP 6.0*), and choose the enhancement package version that you want to install (for example, *SAP Enhancement Package 4 for SAP ERP*) in the TARGET RELEASE VERSION area. Under the SOLUTION AREA selection option, you can limit the functional area for which you want to obtain information (for example, *Human Capital Management*). After you've started the search, the system shows a list of the delta functions in the display area. Using the name of the delta function, you can navigate to the detail view and learn more about the selected function.

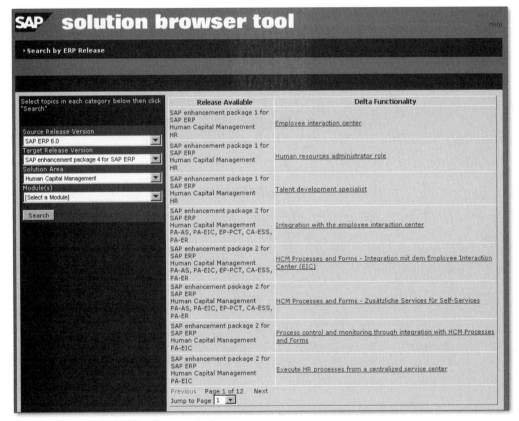

Figure 4.18 Solution Browser Tool

4.6.4 ASU Toolbox

The installation of SAP enhancement packages is accompanied by some application-specific steps before and after the technical installation. The *Application-Specific Upgrade* (ASU) toolbox supports you in determining the steps for this, and executing them in the system in a controlled way. It uses a two-level processing process:

1. In the first step, you load the steps to be processed (ASU content definition) into the SAP system and save them there. The XML file of the ASU content definition is attached to SAP Note 1000009 and can be downloaded there. Using Transaction /n/ASU/START, you then import it into your SAP system.

2. In a subsequent step, a task list is generated from the ASU content definition; this list must then be processed within an enhancement package installation. The task plan contains both *preparation steps* and *follow-up steps*.

For more information on the ASU toolbox, refer to SAP Note 1000009.

4.6.5 Upgrade Dependency Analyzer

The Upgrade Dependency Analyzer (UDA) is an application in the SAP Service Marketplace that shows technical dependencies between system components (product versions) of different release versions. The Upgrade Dependency Analyzer is available in the SAP Service Marketplace at *http://service.sap.com/uda*.

4.6.6 Test Catalogs and Test Case Templates

SAP provides test catalogs for each business function of SAP enhancement packages. These test templates comprise various predefined test cases, so-called test case templates. *End-user tests* are required whenever one or more business functions are activated and thus new business functions are used. Using test case templates, you can test and validate new business functions in a targeted manner. You can supplement and enhance the templates with customer-specific test cases. The test case templates address the following questions:

▶ **Test preparation**
What preparations must be made before a test?

▶ **Test execution**
Which transactions must be executed in which sequence?

▶ **Test result**

How can you evaluate the test result?

You can access the test case templates after the installation of SAP enhancement packages via Transaction SFW5 (see Figure 4.19).

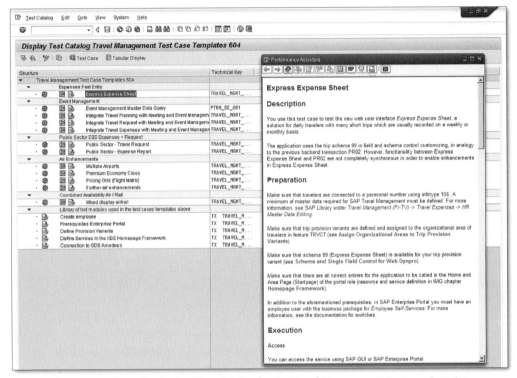

Figure 4.19 Example of a Test Case Catalog for the Travel Management Business Function

Using the TEST CATALOG column, you can navigate to SAP's test case catalog for each business function. You can also download the test case templates via the SAP Service Marketplace at *http://service.sap.com/erp-ehp.* For more information on test case templates, see Chapter 2, Section 2.4, Business Functions, and Chapter 3, Section 3.1.5, Test Management.

> **Note**
>
> A detailed description on how to use a test catalog is available in the SAP Help Portal at *http://help.sap.com* • SAP ERP • SAP ERP ENHANCEMENT PACKAGES • BUSINESS FUNCTIONS (SAP ENHANCEMENT PACKAGE 4 FOR SAP ERP 6.0) • WORKING WITH TEST CASE TEMPLATES.

4.6.7 Switch Framework Cockpit

In SAP Solution Manager, you are provided with an additional function that enables the central management of business function and business function sets for your connected system landscape. Besides the management functions, the Switch Framework cockpit also offers the option to centrally activate business functions and to check the technical interdependencies of business functions. You start the Switch Framework cockpit in your SAP Solution Manager using Transaction SOLMAN_WORKCENTER. Go to the SYSTEM LANDSCAPE MANAGEMENT work center, and select the SWITCH FRAMEWORK COCKPIT entry in the navigation area. The system takes you to the central Switch Framework cockpit, and you can use the SWITCH FRAMEWORK DATE • READ/UPDATE button or view the Switch Framework data of your connected SAP systems. For more information on the Switch Framework cockpit, refer to the SAP Help Portal at *http://help.sap.com* • SAP SOLUTION MANAGER <CURRENT RELEASE> • BASIC SETTINGS • SYSTEM LANDSCAPE SOLUTION MANAGER • SWITCH FRAMEWORK COCKPIT.

4.6.8 Service Offers for Enterprise Support Customers

The service offer *SAP Accelerated Innovation Enablement* (AIE) is part of SAP Enterprise Support. The various parts of this offer are customized for customers who are interested in new functions from SAP enhancement packages and their technical concept. To do this, SAP offers up to five days of remote maintenance service per calendar year, so that you can get information about the new functions. An evaluation of the innovative ability of the latest SAP enhancement packages and their deployment according to your business process requirements are included in this service offer. You can find more information on this service offer and the order process in the SAP Service Marketplace at *http://service.sap.com/enterprisesupport,* and in SAP Note 1300402.

4.6.9 Service Offers from Consulting

SAP Deutschland AG & Co. KG offers its customers a variety of consulting offers and services regarding SAP enhancement packages. The following are two offers from technical consulting.

SAP Enhancement Package Planning for ERP

The *SAP Enhancement Package Planning for ERP* service offer is a consulting offer that is specifically customized to the requirements of SAP customers who are interested in installing SAP enhancement packages. Among other things, the following subject areas are discussed in a two-day workshop held by experienced technical consultants:

▶ Basic principles, technical design, architecture, and Best Practices of SAP enhancement packages for ERP

▶ Usage and role of SAP Solution Manager (system landscape and Maintenance Optimizer) within the scope of an enhancement package project

▶ Project planning, discussion of various project approaches, and creation of a customer-specific roadmap

▶ Identification of relevant business functions and technical usages

▶ Technical dependencies within the SAP system landscape

▶ SAP EHP Installer: functioning and experiences

Customers are provided with a final report that includes a clear summary of the workshop results. After the workshop, SAP can submit an offer for a technical enhancement package installation.

Technical SAP Enhancement Package Coach

The *Technical Enhancement Package Coach* (TEC) is an integral part of your project team and supports you in planning and implementing your enhancement package project. The TEC is an experienced technical consultant who can enriches your installation project with knowledge and experience (Best Practices) he's gained in numerous customer and ramp-up projects. Thanks to a dense network within the SAP organization, additional questions can be addressed in a timely manner. The TEC's fields of activity include the following:

▶ Support in project planning

▶ Quality assurance and project reviews

▶ Support for technical questions and training of administrators for enhancement package installation

▶ Proposals for optimizing the runtime and downtime

▶ Follow-up for support messages and open questions

▶ Support in the creation of a cutover planning for the transition weekend

You will be sent a customer-specific offer after a preliminary telephone discussion. For more information on the consulting offers and the order, refer to *http://service. sap.com/ufg*; you can also send an inquiry to *upgradecc@sap.com*.

This chapter provides many useful tips and experiences to help keep your enhancement package projects running smoothly.

5   Practical Experience and Tips on Enhancement Package Installations

Chapter 4, Implementation Tools and Service Offers, discussed enhancement package installation tools and service offers in detail. This chapter provides real-life experiences to help support the technical implementation of your enhancement package installation. This chapter is a supplement to the documentation already available in the SAP Service Marketplace, and the tips presented here refer to the topics discussed in Chapter 4 (for example, SAP Solution Manager and EHP Installer). Background information on the analysis and optimization of enhancement package installations is also included. Finally, the chapter provides additional information on switching business functions, taking into account important aspects that should be considered in the process.

5.1   Useful Tips on SAP Solution Manager

SAP Solution Manager is the tool you use to prepare every enhancement package installation for SAP ERP. Besides the information on the system landscape, you also use the Maintenance Optimizer for selecting and downloading SAP enhancement packages. In this chapter, we focus on the problems and questions that we've often encountered in our day-to-day project work, and outline possible approaches and solution options.

5.1.1   Updating Product Data in SAP Solution Manager

The Maintenance Optimizer requires current product data to provide you with the most current enhancement package releases. If you operate your SAP Solution Manager with a support package version below SP19, you must import the product data manually into SAP Solution Manager (as of SP19 the current product data is provided). If no current product data is available, the system provides the following error message in the maintenance transaction: "Update the product data in SAP Solution Manager!" In documentation and SAP notes, this product data is also referred to as *Product and Production Management System (PPMS) data*. Therefore, import the product data into your SAP Solution Manager before you create a new maintenance transaction. The PPMS data is provided as XML files and imported into the system via the RS_SMSY_PPMS_XML_UP_DOWNLOAD report using the UPLOAD = 'X' option. SAP Note 1277035 provides instructions and a ZIP archive with the required XML data.

5.1.2 Practical Approach for Selecting Relevant Technical Usages

SAP recommends importing SAP enhancement packages within the scope of a regular maintenance activity in an SAP ERP system. This means that the installation queue is comprised of enhancement packages and the current support package stack, and is imported using the EHP Installer installation tool.

Installation Queue

The term *installation queue* (also referred to as *package queue* or *import queue*) refers to the set of support package and enhancement package bundles that the Maintenance Optimizer calculated in the maintenance transaction for your enhancement package installation. You install the installation queue using EHP Installer. The packages of the installation queue are listed in the package configuration file (stack XML), amongst others.

The right half of Figure 5.1 shows the new lifecycle of SAP applications compared to the traditional lifecycle (left half of the figure), which is a sequence of upgrades and maintenance activities.

Another recommendation by SAP relates to the selective installation of enhancement packages. As you've already learned in Chapter 2, Architecture and Technology, enhancement packages include new versions of software components. You select them using the technical usage, and the selection should correspond to the actual requirement for new functionality. This means that you don't need to install the full scope of an SAP enhancement package, but only selected parts. This approach reduces the technical installation effort with regard to installation runtime. Considered separately, the two recommendations are inherently consistent and feasible. Frequently, this recommendation results in the following question: Which parts of an SAP enhancement package, or which technical usages, are supposed to be installed if no concrete business demand for new functions exists yet, but you still want to be prepared for future (or even short-term) demands?

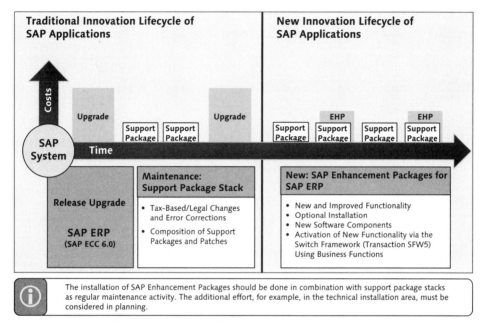

The installation of SAP Enhancement Packages should be done in combination with support package stacks as regular maintenance activity. The additional effort, for example, in the technical installation area, must be considered in planning.

Figure 5.1 Traditional and New Lifecycle of SAP Applications

This question refers directly to the results of the *Requirements* project phase mentioned in Chapter 3, Section 3.3, Enhancement Package Project Phases and Activities. Importing enhancement packages outside the regular maintenance window is not feasible for a lot of customers because it entails, in addition to other influencing factors, locking the development environment, retesting, and additional system downtime.

The following sections discuss how to select the "appropriate" technical usages for an SAP ERP system (SAP ECC Server). This approach is also referred to as a *broad approach,* and is illustrated in Figure 5.2.

Selecting the Required Core Function

Question: Which core function do you use in your SAP ERP system?

The *Central Applications* technical usage includes the software components SAP_ APPL and EA-APPL. These software components are comprised of, among others, core functions such as Material Management (MM), Controlling (CO), Financial Accounting (FI), Sales and Distribution (SD), Quality Management (QM), and Project System (PS). Select the Central Applications technical usage if you want to implement new functions in one of these areas.

1 Selection of the Required Core Function:		
Technical Usage(s)	Central Applications	Human Capital Management

2 Plus **Optional** Selection of the Enhanced Function:				
Technical Usage(s)	ERecruiting on ECC Server	HCM—Learning Solution	Global Trade	Financial Supply Chain Mgmt.
	ESA ECC-SE	PLM Core	Financial Services	

3 Plus **Optional** Selection of **One** Industry-Specific Technical Usage:				
Technical Usage(s)	Discrete Ind. & Mill Products	Oil & Gas	Hospital	Public Sector Accounting
	Catch Weight Management	Insurance	Media	Utilities/Waste&Recycl./Telco
	Oil& Gas with Utilities	Retail	Defense	Defense Forces & Public Sec.
	Financials—Contr. Acc. & Leasing			

Figure 5.2 Broad Approach for Selecting the Relevant Technical Usages

The *Human Capital Management* technical usage includes the software components SAP_HR and EA-HR. These software components are comprised of functions such as Personnel Management, Personnel Time Management and Payroll, and national specifics of various countries. Select the *Human Capital Management* technical usage if you want to implement new functions in human resources (HR).

Optional Selection of the Enhanced Function

Question: Do you use enhanced functions?

Log on to your SAP ERP system, and start Transaction SPRO. In the Implementation Guide (IMG), select Activate Business Functions. You can also use Transaction SFW5. The initial screen of the Switch Framework opens (see Figure 5.3).

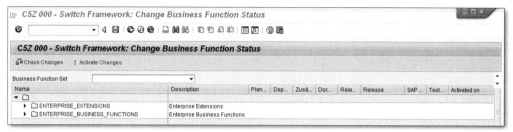

Figure 5.3 Initial Screen of the Switch Framework (Transaction SFW5)

Open the ENTERPRISE_EXTENSIONS folder. You can now view a list of enterprise extensions for your SAP ERP system. Extensions that are switched on are indicated with a yellow bulb (see Figure 5.4).

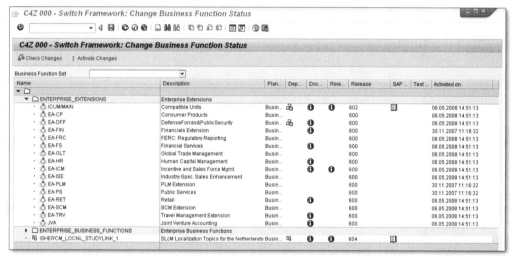

Figure 5.4 Switched On Enterprise Extensions of an SAP ERP System

Note the switched on enterprise extensions. Based on Table 5.1, you can determine which software component the switched on extensions belong to (including examples of which technical usage contains this software component). For more information, see SAP Note 658351.

Enterprise Extensions	Description	Assigned Software Component	Technical Usage*
EA-CP	Consumer Products	EA-APPL	Central Applications
EA-FIN	Financials Extension	EA-APPL	Central Applications
EA-FRC	FERC: Regulatory Reporting	EA-FINSERV	Financial Services
EA-FS	Financial Services	EA-FINSERV	Financial Services
EA-GLT	Global Trade Management	EA-GLTRADE	Global Trade
EA-HR	Human Capital Management	EA-HR	Human Capital Management
EA-ICM	Incentive and Sales Force Management	EA-APPL	Central Applications
EA-ISE	Industry-Specific Sales Extension	EA-APPL	Central Applications
EA-PLM	Product Lifecycle Management (PLM) Extension	EA-APPL	Central Applications
EA-SCM	Supply Chain Management (SCM) Extension	EA-APPL	Central Applications
EA-TRV	Travel Management Extension	EA-HR	Human Capital Management and HCM – Travel Management
JVA	Joint Venture Accounting	EA-APPL	Central Applications
*Multiple technical usages can contain the same software component; this table only presents one possible assignment.			

Table 5.1 Assigning Enterprise Extensions to Software Components

In principle, you are not required to bring the software components of the active enterprise extension to a higher version as long as no dependent industry solution is switched on. Instead, this approach gives you the option of identifying already-used functions without exactly knowing the customer-specific processes.

However, this presupposes that the enterprise extensions were switched on deliberately and the functional extension is actually used. The obvious conclusion is to provide new functionality for these enterprise extensions. You can identify the corresponding technical usages based on the mapping report that is attached to SAP Note 1165438 (for enhancement package 4).

Example

You've switched on the EA-FIN and EA-FS enterprise extensions. These functions are located in the EA-FINSERV software component. The EA-FINSERV software component, in turn, is part of the *Financial Services* technical usage, and can thus be a possible selection in the maintenance transaction of the Maintenance Optimizer.

If no enterprise extensions should be switched on in your system, you still have the option of using enhanced SAP functionality; for example, E-Recruiting (technical usage: *ERecruiting on ECC Server*, software component: ERECRUIT) or Learning Solution (technical usage: *Human Capital Management – Learning Solution*, software component: LSOFE). Ask your IT department to see if this function is already in use or is supposed to be used in the future.

Optional Selection of One Industry-Specific Technical Usage

Question: Is an industry solution activated?

Transaction SFW5 checks to see if an industry solution is active. If this is the case, the switched on industry solution must be considered in the technical usage selection in the Maintenance Optimizer (because activated industry solutions must always be updated in the enhancement package installation according to the enhancement package rules). The technical usage of a switched on industry solution is automatically selected by the Maintenance Optimizer.

Example

Assume you've activated the industry solution *IS-Automotive* (ECC-DIMP) in your system; therefore, you must select the *Discrete Industries & Mill Products* technical usage in the maintenance transaction. This selection ensures that besides the SAP_APPL and EA-APPL software components, you also bring the industry-specific software component, ECC-DIMP, to a current version. Switched on industry solutions must always be imported within the scope of an enhancement package installation.

Additional Approaches for Selecting Relevant Technical Usages

To supplement the broad approach, consider the following questions when selecting additional technical usages.

▸ *Has an older version of an SAP enhancement package been installed?*
Log on to your SAP ERP system, and select the STATUS entry via the SYSTEM menu. Check the version of the individual software components. If application-related software components should have a version higher than 600 (for example, version 602 or 603), they must be updated. In this context, also refer to Chapter 2, Section 2.2.3, Prerequisites for the Installation of an Enhancement Package. Based on the *mapping report,* you can derive the possible assignments of these software components from the technical usages. The Maintenance Optimizer usually indicates the required technical usages automatically if an older enhancement package version is already installed.

▸ *Which business functions can supplement your existing processes?*
Ask the application managers to determine, based on the documentation of your core processes, whether these can be supplemented or reasonably enhanced with new functions from the enhancement packages. Here, the application manager should roughly specify the functional requirements; a mapping of business functions to technical usages is not required.

▸ *Are there custom developments that can be replaced by a new function of an SAP enhancement package?*
Another way to define the relevant technical usages is to check your custom developments. Consult with your user departments to see if SAP enhancement packages contain functions that could replace your custom developments (or planned custom developments).

5.1.3 Selecting the "Correct" Product Version

SAP enhancement package 4 for SAP ERP provides two different product versions:

1. Enhancement package 4 for SAP ERP 6.0

2. Enhancement package 4 for SAP ERP 6.0/NW 7.01

You can use these product versions to obtain various enhancement package 4–based target statuses in your landscape. The following sections discuss these options.

SAP ERP 6.0 (SAP ECC Server)

The selection of the product version doesn't matter in a pure ABAP-based system. For both product versions, enhancement package 1 for SAP NetWeaver 7.0 is imported into the SAP ERP 6.0 system (SAP ECC Server) in an enhancement package 4 installation. After an enhancement package 4 installation, the target status of SAP NetWeaver is always SAP NetWeaver 7.01.

Java-Based System Components

If you operate Java-based system components in the landscape for which the enhancement package 4 functionality is provided, the selection of the product version plays a decisive role. In principle, you can select which target status of SAP NetWeaver is supposed to be achieved. The following SAP NetWeaver target statuses are possible:

▶ SAP NetWeaver 7.0 (corresponds to product version enhancement package 4 for SAP ERP 6.0)

▶ SAP NetWeaver 7.01 (corresponds to product version enhancement package 4 for SAP ERP 6.0/NW 7.01)

Additional Modeling Options

The *content* is another part of the enhancement package 4 function. Enhancement package 4–specific content is provided for the following SAP products:

▶ **SAP NetWeaver Business Warehouse (BW) 7.0**
The Business Intelligence (BI) content (technical name: BI-Cont 704) can be installed in SAP NetWeaver 7.0 or SAP NetWeaver 7.01 within the scope of an enhancement package 4 installation.

▶ **SAP NetWeaver Portal 7.0**
The portal content can be installed in SAP NetWeaver 7.0 or SAP NetWeaver 7.01 within the scope of an enhancement package 4 installation.

▶ **SAP NetWeaver Process Integration (PI) 7.0**
PI content packages are provided for specific software components, which are summarized in the *Standard XI Content* technical usage.

Figure 5.5 shows the different selection options.

Summary

▶ Use *enhancement package 4 for SAP ERP 6.0* product version if you want to update Java-based product instances of your SAP ERP 6.0 landscape without enhancement package 1 for SAP NetWeaver 7.0.

▶ Use *enhancement package 4 for SAP ERP 6.0/NW 7.01* product version if you want to update Java-based product instances of your SAP ERP 6.0 landscape with enhancement package 1 for SAP NetWeaver 7.0.

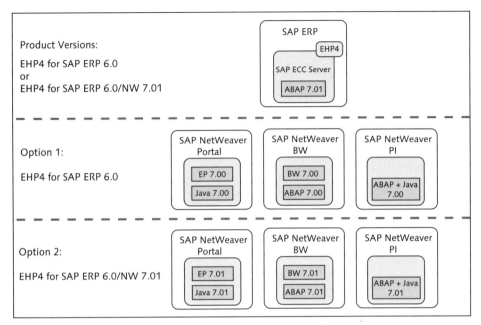

Figure 5.5 Selection Options in an Enhancement Package 4 Installation

5.1.4 Special Features of the Package Configuration Files

This chapter not only presents the *system-specific* package configuration file (stack XML), but also the *cross-system and cross-landscape* package configuration file (cross XML).

System-Specific and Cross-System Package Configuration Files

In the Maintenance Optimizer, you can create maintenance transactions for SAP systems of a product version that are assigned to a logical component. In one of the first steps of the maintenance transaction, you have the option of selecting one or more systems for your landscape and the system then generates a package configuration file.

The following text describes an example that highlights the differences between the package configuration files. Let's assume a classical three-level SAP ERP system landscape, including a development system (DEV), a quality assurance system (QAS), and a production system (PRD). You can select from the following options to plan the maintenance:

▶ You generate a separate maintenance transaction for each system of your landscape and get a total of *three* package configuration files (stack XMLs) for your landscape (file name: SMSDXML_<SID>_<DATE, TIME>.XML).

▶ You generate one maintenance transaction for all systems of your landscape and obtain *one* package configuration file. This cross-system package configuration file is also referred to as *cross XML* (file name: SMSDXML_CROSSSYS_<DATE, TIME>.XML).

Figure 5.6 shows the two options.

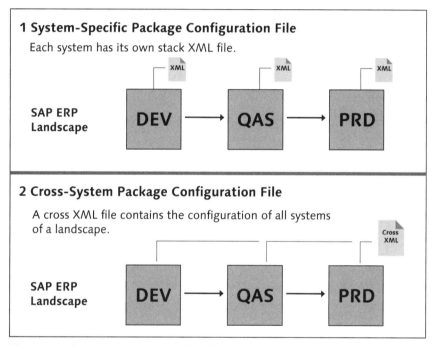

Figure 5.6 Comparing System-specific and Cross-system Package Configuration Files

A cross XML file includes the packages of the installation queue for the selected systems of your landscape; in this example, for the DEV, QAS, and PRD systems. The benefit of a cross XML file is that the target status, which comprises the selection of the highest support package stack and your selection of the technical usages, is identical for all systems of your three-level SAP ERP landscape after the installation. This reduces the user errors that can occur when manually selecting the target status in the Maintenance Optimizer. A cross XML file contains three system-specific sections in case of a three-level system landscape. In other words:

A cross XML file consists of three system-specific stack XML files that are "lined up" in a package configuration file. Therefore, the systems wouldn't have to have a uniform initial status, because the package calculation would still be for each system individually (see Figure 5.7). If a cross XML file is created for a landscape, the initial status of the system doesn't have to be changed (for example, by importing support packages or add-on products).

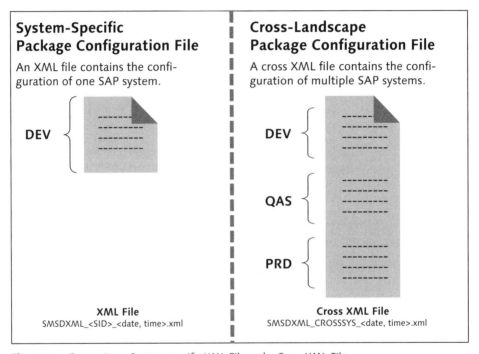

Figure 5.7 Comparing a System-specific XML File and a Cross XML File

Cross-Landscape Package Configuration Files

At the beginning of this chapter, the term *cross-landscape package configuration file* was introduced; let's discuss this concept in more detail. A cross-landscape package configuration file can comprise the installation queues of multiple SAP ERP systems (SAP ECC Server) of a landscape *and* additional product instances that run on SAP NetWeaver 7.0. To do this, refer to Section 5.1.3, Selecting the "Correct" Product Version, which presents the various product versions and the related landscape options. For example, you can select technical usages for your SAP ERP system (SAP ECC Server), and enhancement package 4 parts for your SAP NetWeaver Portal (such as portal content). In this example, the maintenance transaction would generate a cross XML file, which you could use for installing the two system landscapes (see Figure 5.8).

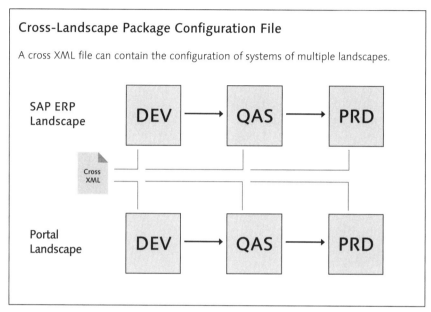

Figure 5.8 Example of a Cross XML File with Cross-landscape Enhancement Package 4 Components

5.1.5 Checking the Consistency of the Installation Queue

An installation queue can consist of support packages and enhancement package subsets. The Maintenance Optimizer automatically calculates this installation queue based on your entries in the maintenance transaction. Here, it is ensured that the installation queue itself is consistent (i.e., that the technical interdependency of the packages is ensured). However, you can individually change the automatically calculated queue by adding or deselecting packages. For example, you can remove support packages for unused industry components from the installation queue. Therefore, in the maintenance transaction, you are provided with an option to recheck your installation queue for consistency prior to download. You can execute this critical check function at the end of the maintenance transaction by clicking the CHECK VALID support package stack ENHANCEMENT PACKAGE QUEUE button.

5.1.6 Deselecting Packages of the Installation Queue

Section 5.1.5, Checking the Consistency of the Installation Queue, already mentioned that you have the option of deselecting individual packages from the installation queue. Customers have often asked which packages they can deselect and whether the deselection of individual packages makes sense at all.

Purpose

To begin, let's consider the benefits of deselecting individual packages of the installation queue. An argument in favor of deselecting individual support packages is the technical import time and system downtime that results from importing packages. The basic rule here is that the more support package and enhancement package subsets that are available in the installation queue and imported into your system, the longer the whole import runtime and downtime takes. However, the overall import runtime of an enhancement package installation does not increase just because of the number of packages. Ultimately, many factors are at work; for example, the number of objects in a package, and the level of parallelization during the import of packages.

Options

Deselecting enhancement packages does not make sense and can lead to errors. Only selected enhancement packages should be in the installation queue, along with new software components that technically depend on you select; for example, the new software component, SAP Business Suite Foundation (SAP_BS_Foundation, technical: SAP_BS_FND), which is part of an enhancement package 4 installation.

Enhancement package 4 for SAP ERP is a delta delivery for enhancement package 3 for SAP ERP. Therefore, you can always find enhancement package 3–specific *and* enhancement package 4–specific packages in your installation queue in an enhancement package 4 installation. (Exception: If you've already installed enhancement package 3 in your SAP system, you only need to install the delta packages of enhancement package 4.) The bottom line is: never deselect enhancement packages in your installation queue! Restrict the deselection of packages to support packages for SAP industry solutions. You must import support packages of an industry solution whenever the following rules apply:

- An industry solution is switched on in your SAP system.
- You intend to switch on an industry solution at a later point in time.
- A technical dependency exists (very rare).

Check to see if an industry solution is activated in your system (Transaction SFW5). If this is the case, you can deselect all support packages for industry solutions that are not switched on (in an SAP ERP system, only one industry business function set can be activated at a time). If no industry solution is switched on in your system, you must check to see if an activation would even be possible at a later point in time due to business or functional requirements. You can deselect all of those industry-specific support packages for which a future use is excluded. After you've deselected packages, you should always use the CHECK VALID SPS & ENHANCEMENT PACKAGE QUEUE option (as described in Section 5.1.5, Checking the Consistency of the Installation Queue). For further information on support package stack strategy, visit the SAP Service Marketplace at *http://service.sap.com/sp-stacks* • DETAILS ON THE COMPONENTS OF A SP STACK.

Additional Information: Determining Technical Import Conditions

You can find technical dependencies of support packages, also referred to as *import conditions*, in the SAP Service Marketplace at *http://service.sap.com/swdc*. Follow the DOWNLOAD • SUPPORT PACKAGES AND PATCHES • SEARCH FOR SUPPORT PACKAGES AND PATCHES menu path from the navigation area on the left.

Here, we discuss this procedure based on the FINSERV enterprise extensions. To do this, enter "EA-FINSERV" in the search field, and start the search. From the search results, select the required EA-FINSERV component version; for example, EA-FINSERV 600. The system opens a new window to display the available support packages. Go to the entry of the highest support package version (for example, SP16 for EA-FINSERV 6.00), and click the INFO link in the INFO FILE column. A new window opens where you can now view the technical details on Support Package 16; for example, the package name (SAPKGPFD16) and various package attributes.

Now select the first import condition (1ST IMPORT CONDITION) in the PACKAGE IMPORT CONDITIONS column, and confirm your selection using the arrow button (>>). The system opens a new window to display the import conditions and additional information (see Figure 5.9).

MAIN COMPONENTS			SUPPORT PACKAGES	
Component	Release	Value	Package	Value
SAP_APPL	600	T	SAPKGPFD15	T
			SAPKH60016	T

ADD-ON COMPONENTS			OTHER CONDITIONS		
Add-On	Release	Value	Component	Release	Value
EA-FINSERV	600	T	-		

All Conditions Must Be Met Simultaneously!

Figure 5.9 Import Conditions and Technical Dependency of SP16 of Enterprise Extension EA-FINSERV

You can derive the following information from this detail view:

▶ The SAP_APPL software component is the *main component* of the EA-FINSERV enterprise extension.

▶ Packages SP15 for EA-FINSERV 600 (SAPKGPFD15) and SP16 for SAP_APPL 600 (SAPKH60016) are the required support packages of SP16 for EA-FINSERV 600.

So, on the one hand, Support Package SP16 for EA-FINSERV 6.00 is an import condition itself; in other words, to import SP16, SP15 must either already be installed in your SAP system or be part of the installation queue. (Support packages are based on one another and are not cumulative.)

On the other hand, the SAP_APPL software component is the *main component* of the EA-FINSERV enterprise extension. Therefore, the EA-FINSERV enterprise extension technically depends on the SAP_APPL software component. Support Package SP16 for SAP_APPL 600 must either be installed in the SAP system already or be part of the installation queue.

5.1.7 Additional Documentation

At this point, we'd like to draw your attention to some additional documentation that can support you in configuring SAP Solution Manager.

▶ **Create systems**
The online documentation for SAP Solution Manager is available in the SAP Help Portal. Here you can find, among other things, step-by-step instructions and additional information on creating systems (Transaction SMSY).

Select the SAP SOLUTION MANAGER menu entry at *http://help.sap.com*. Open the documentation in your preferred language. In the menu structure via the BASIC SETTINGS • SAP SOLUTION MANAGER SYSTEM LANDSCAPE • CREATE SYSTEMS menu path, you can find detailed descriptions; FOR EXAMPLE, descriptions about generating remote function call (RFC) connections, creating Java systems, or changing the assignment of a system to a product version.

▶ **Create transactions**
The SAP Help Portal also provides step-by-step instructions for creating maintenance transactions using SAP enhancement packages at *http://help.sap.com* • SAP SOLUTION MANAGER • BASIC SETTINGS • CHANGE REQUEST MANAGEMENT AND CHANGE CONTROL • MAINTENANCE OPTIMIZER • MAINTENANCE transaction SCENARIOS • MAINTENANCE TRANSACTION WITH INSTALLATION OF AN ENHANCEMENT PACKAGE.

The SAP Service Marketplace provides other useful documentation:

▶ How to exchange system data between SMSY and System Landscape Directory (SLD)

▶ How to configure Maintenance Optimizer to use Software Lifecycle Manager (SLM)

▶ SAP Solution Manager in a high-security infrastructure (describes the use of the Maintenance Optimizers without a remote connection to SAP)

You can find these documents in the SAP Service Marketplace at *http://service.sap.com/solutionmanager* • MEDIA LIBRARY • HOW-TO DOCUMENTS. Moreover, SAP Note 1122966 lists the essential SAP notes that will be imported in SAP Solution Manager prior to an enhancement package installation.

5.2 Useful Tips on EHP Installer

The goal of this section is to provide you with some useful tips on handling SAP EHP Installer, focusing on only the most commonly encountered topics or problem situations. The sequence of the sections is based on the order of an enhancement package installation.

5.2.1 Additional Documentation and Information

SAP provides various technical documentations that you should read carefully prior to installation, and that you should always have readily available during an installation. Reading the documents will help you implement the technical installation successfully. The following briefly outlines the most important documents:

- **How to Install EHP4: A Practical Guide**
  This how-to guide covers the holistic implementation cycle of SAP enhancement packages from the relevant settings in Solution Manager, to the EHP Installer start process, to useful links and tips. This useful document includes numerous supplementary descriptions on enhancement package topics, and solutions on frequently occurring problems. The document is available at *http://service.sap.com/erp-inst* • SAP ENHANCEMENT PACKAGES FOR SAP ERP 6.0 • SAP ENHANCEMENT PACKAGE 4 FOR SAP ERP 6.0.

- **SAP Enhancement Package Installation Guide**
  The technical EHP Installer guide helps you through the individual steps of the technical installation of SAP enhancement packages and describes the technical preparations, the installation process, and the necessary technical postprocessing. You should *read* this document *carefully* before you start the installation, and use it during the installation as a guide through the individual installation phases and dialog prompts. It includes helpful background information on many issues; for example, on modifying and resetting installations. The guide is available at *http://service.sap.com/erp-inst* • SAP ENHANCEMENT PACKAGES FOR SAP ERP 6.0 • SAP ENHANCEMENT PACKAGE 4 FOR SAP ERP 6.0 • ENHANCEMENT PACKAGE INSTALLATION ON EXISTING SAP SYSTEMS • SAP ENHANCEMENT PACKAGE INSTALLATION ON ABAP SYSTEMS (USING SAPEHPI).

  Then select your combination of operating system and database. Special guides are also available that describe an installation using Transaction SAINT (mandatory for 32-bit platforms).

- **Troubleshooting and Administration Guide**
  The Troubleshooting and Administration Guide is based on installations using EHP Installer. It comprises a list of frequent errors that occur in the various installation phases, and the appropriate solutions. This documentation is supplemented with a chapter that focuses on topics like optimization approaches of technical downtime, tool parameters, and other details. After you've extracted the EHP Installer SAR archive, you can find the Troubleshooting Guide in your installation directory under EHPI/ABAP/HTDOC.

- **Central SAP Notes for SAP Enhancement Packages for SAP ERP 6.0**
  This central notes page features a very clear structure and facilitates navigation through essential notes on the enhancement package installation. You can find

the central enhancement package note pages at *http://service.sap.com/erp-inst* • SAP ERP 6.0 • SAP ENHANCEMENT PACKAGES FOR SAP ERP 6.0 • SAP NOTES (ENHANCEMENT PACKAGES).

▶ **Technical FAQ for EHP4**

This document contains the customers' most frequently asked questions on the enhancement package topic. The document is available at *http://service.sap.com/erp-inst* • SAP ENHANCEMENT PACKAGES FOR SAP ERP 6.0 • SAP ENHANCEMENT PACKAGE 4 FOR SAP ERP 6.0.

▶ **SAP Note 1311835**

SAP Note 1311835 provides information on the delta sizing of enhancement package 4 for SAP ERP.

▶ **Training offering**

You can get information on SAP's training offering at *www.sap.com/usa/education*. The new two-day training, ADM327 — Enhancement Package Installation, addresses the target group of system administrators, technical consultants, and project team leads who want to learn more about the technical background and implementation of an enhancement package installation in real life.

5.2.2   Installation Cookbook

The installation cookbook is the most valuable working document for an administrator who carries out technical enhancement package installations.

Purpose

The main purpose of creating an installation cookbook is to ensure a smooth technical installation in the production system. You should invest an appropriate amount of time and effort in the creation and maintenance of this installation cookbook; keep in mind, though, it should not be a copy of the existing SAP installation guides, but rather a working guide that is compiled specifically for you and documents every technical step, as little as it may be. It is created for the first technical installation (in a sandbox system) and optimized and completed with every additional installation. The cookbook will eventually replace SAP's technical EHP Installation Guide. Many customers consider the creation of an installation cookbook an inherent part of every technical project; however, there are also project situations in which an installation cookbook has little or no meaning at all, or whose documentation quality is poor.

Structure of the Cookbook

A good installation cookbook should always be designed in such a way that it provides all essential information in a way that is easy to navigate. It is up to you whether to select a document template that is based on a spreadsheet calculation or word processing program. However, the basic structure should be subdivided into the following areas:

- Documentation of technical preparations
- Documentation of the tool-based installation, if required, subdivided into installation uptime and installation downtime
- Documentation of technical postprocessing

Time information on the duration of the respective activities and information on the date and time is a useful supplement.

After completing the first installation, you can check the exact runtime of the installation phases in the runtime analysis file, UPGANA.XML (see Section 5.3.3, Runtime Analysis File of an Enhancement Package Installation). Because you also use the installation cookbook for subsequent installations, we recommend that you use a status field for each work step. This way, you will know at a glance whether a specific activity was done or not (this is particularly important for handling technical preparations and postprocessing).

The individual work steps should always be sorted chronologically and in blocks within the basic structure. For example, you can subdivide the "technical preparations" block into database-specific, operating system–specific, and SAP system–specific activities. A second chronological outline level is useful; for example, by work steps that can be carried out a couple of days or weeks in advance. It's a question of taste whether you want to create an installation cookbook that includes screenshots. If you save screenshots, you must consider the image format: The graphic formats GIF and PNG are recommended because both use a lossless image compression. If you don't want to type the installation dialog text, you can find the text in the SAPehpiConsole.log file in the EHPI/ABAP/LOG directory during installation, where you can copy it to your installation cookbook. The individual dialog inputs are also stored there.

Figure 5.10 shows an excerpt of the SAPehpiConsole.log file. The file contains a date and exact time, which document an installation phase started in, and when it was completed. Besides the phase's name, it also lists the complete dialog texts and your entries. In this example, the dialog prompt was answered with Yes.

```
>> 2009/07/14 08:57:17   START OF PHASE PREP_EXTENSION/PATCHK_EQUI

>> 2009/07/14 08:57:18   END OF PHASE    PREP_EXTENSION/PATCHK_EQUI


>> 2009/07/14 08:57:18   START OF PHASE PREP_EXTENSION/PATCH_CHK3

>> 2009/07/14 08:57:26   END OF PHASE    PREP_EXTENSION/PATCH_CHK3


>> 2009/07/14 08:57:26   START OF PHASE PREP_EXTENSION/BIND_PATCH

You can include Support Packages of the target release.
You need this if the current package level can only be retained
with equivalent Support Packages of the target release.

Do you want to include (further) Support Packages of the target release?

            - "Yes"
            - "No"

Enter one of these options [Yes] := Yes
Uploading data ...
According to the uploaded packages the queue calculator
could generate a valid support package queue.

>> 2009/07/14 09:18:40   END OF PHASE    PREP_EXTENSION/BIND_PATCH


>> 2009/07/14 09:18:40   START OF PHASE PREP_EXTENSION/COMPINFO_SPP

>> 2009/07/14 09:18:41   END OF PHASE    PREP_EXTENSION/COMPINFO_SPP
```

Figure 5.10   Excerpt of the SAPehpiConsole.log Installation Log File

Practical Tips

Experience has shown that high-quality and complete documentation must always be created in parallel to the installation. Documenting the work after the fact runs the risk of critical information or error solutions being only partially entered or not at all. With regard to content, the installation cookbook should consist of concise, but significant and comprehensible instructions. Remarks on what needs to be considered in follow-up installations are also helpful.

If errors occur during installation, the complete solution path should be documented, even if you can no longer identify precisely which step ultimately led to the solution; this way, you can determine the correct solution path in follow-up installations. You revise and supplement the installation cookbook with every installation so that you have a complete documentation of all activities, dialog inputs, and solution paths for known errors for the installation in production. The following figures present two different examples of installation cookbooks. Both cookbooks feature a clear structure and — thanks to the exact instructions — enable third parties to understand the required activities (see Figures 5.11 and 5.12).

Start	Duration	Status	Phase	Activities	Comment
Manual Preparation					
				General Preparations	
		Info	Manual Preparation	SAP EHP Installer Documentation	Path: http://service.sap.com/erp-inst
		Info	Manual Preparation	Important SAP Documentations	How to install EHP4: A Practical Guide, http://service.sap.com/eph-inst
		Info	Manual Preparation	General SAP Note	Note 1143022
		Info	Manual Preparation	SAPehpi specific Note	Note 1245473 (Tool Version 7.00)
		OK	Manual Preparation	**Prepare free space for EHP4 installation**	free space for shadow instance: ~100 GB free space for download directory: ~10 GB free space for EHPI installation directory: ~ 25 GB prepare free space in DB specific archive directory (e.g. /oraarch) prepare free space in /usr/sap/trans directory ~ some GB
		open	Manual Preparation	Create directory on central installation server	create download directory (e.g. download_EHP4) mkdir download_EHP4 and fill with EHP4 files, EHP Installer tool, latest 7.00 Kernel and XML file required space ~ 30 GB (depends on amount of EHP4 files & SPS) Further Support Packs should be as well in this directory (e.g. for Add Ons)
		open	Manual Preparation	Select required Technical Usage in MOPZ Maintenance Transaction:	**Required EHP4 Technical Usages (broad selection):** 1. ESA ECC-SE (Enterprise Services) (ESA ECC-SE 604) 2. Central Application (SAP_APPL und EA_APPL) 3. Financial Services (SAP_APPL 6.04 und EA-FINSERV 604) 4. Insurance (SAP_APPL 6.04, FI-CA 604, INSURANCE 604) 5. EAM Config Control (EA-IPPE 404) 6. Financial Supply Chain Mgmt (FINBASIS) 7. Financials (Leasing/Contract A/R & A/P (FI-CAX)
		Info	Manual Preparation	Following support packs were deselected during download of EHP4:	I EA-DFPS SP 04-15 I EA-PS SP 04-15 I EA-GLTRADE SP 04-15 I EA-RETAIL SP 04-15 I LSOFE (FRONT END) SP 04 -15 I ERECRUIT SP 04-15
				Download EHP Components (via MOPZ, Selection of technical Usage) and XML stack file	TA SMSY & TA MOPZ Copy download to "download directory" e.g. download_EHP4
				Names of XML Stack files for ERP landscape	
				Download latest version of EHP Installer Tool	Path: http://service.sap.com/swdc --> Entry by Application Group --> Additional Components --> Upgrade Tools --> SAP EHP Installer --> SAP EHP Installer 7.00 --> Download OS specific tool
				Download JCE Policy file: "SAP Java Cryptography Extension Jurisdiction Policy"	Download path in SAP Note: 1240081 http://service.sap.com/swdc/download --> SAP Cryptographic Software copy to download directory on central instance host Further information, note: 1238121 DO not extract ZIP Archive!
				Check free space of server file systems	free space for shadow instance: ~100 GB free space for download directory: ~20 GB free space for /usr/sap/trans/EPS/in directory: ~15 GB prepare free space in DB specific archive directory (e.g. /oraarch)
				Execute SAPehpi tool as user <sid> adm	this creates the installation directory "EHPI" with several subdirectorys copy JCE Policy file in this EHPI directory

Figure 5.11 Excerpt of an Installation Cookbook in Table Form

When you implement an enhancement package installation for the first time, you must take into account the time and effort required in creating an installation cookbook, and the maintenance and adaptation effort that arises over the course of the project. However, the benefits of an installation cookbook are quickly evident. For example, the greatest benefit can be found not only in the exact description of the individual activities, but also in considerable time savings in all follow-up installations, because the activities can be processed chronologically. Over the course of an installation, make sure you indicate which activities can be prepared prior to the installation's start. An estimate of what time dialog prompts are to be expected can help you to optimize the entire installation procedure with regard to time (because usually the next dialog prompt appears a few minutes after you've closed the work center). Because installing SAP enhancement packages can repeat itself in subsequent maintenance projects, a well-managed installation cookbook can be a major benefit later on.

Technical documentation of EHP4 installation, SAP System <SID>   <Author>

3.2.1 Create Download directory

```
cd /home/ehp_tmp/<SID>/
mkdir download
chown <SID>adm:sapsys download
chmod 775 download
```

Status: ok

3.2.2 Check DB inconsistency

```
Transaction code DB02
> Diagnostics
> Missing Tables and Indexes
> Button: Refresh
```

Result of consistency check: no inconsistent table or indexes.
start: 04.03.2010, 8:00 am // end: 04.03.2010, 8:05 am // duration: 00:05 h

Status: ok

3.2.3 Create statistics

```
su - <SID>adm -c "brconnect -u / -c -f stats -t oradict_stats"
su - <SID>adm -c "brconnect -u / -c -f stats -t system_stats"
su - <SID>adm -c "brconnect -u / -c -f stats -t all -f collect -p 12"
```

start: 04.03.2010, 8:05 am // end: 04.03.2010, 8:35 am // duration: 00:30 h

Status: ok

Figure 5.12 Excerpt of an Installation Cookbook in Text Form

5.2.3 Parallel Enhancement Package Installations on a Physical Host

This section provides an example of a customer situation, describes the resulting problems, and indicates a solution. The scenario is as follows: Multiple SAP central instances are operated on one physical host, and enhancement package installations are supposed to be performed for the respective systems on these central instances. What factors need to be considered here?

Flexible Assignment of Port Numbers of EHP Installer

Chapter 4, Section 4.5.6, Communication Routine, already discussed how communication is set up between the SL Controller server program and the SDT GUI frontend tool. EHP Installer (or more precisely, SL Controller) uses up to four different ports for the communication routine:

▶ **HTTP port (default port 4239)**
The HTTP port is used for communicating via an HTTP frontend (for example, Internet Explorer) with SL Controller.

▶ **GUI port (default port 4241)**
The GUI port is used for communicating between the SDT GUI user interface and the SL Controller.

▶ **ABAP tool port SAPehpi (default port 4240)**
The ABAP tool port SAPehpi is used for communication between SL Controller and the SAPehpi ABAP program.

▶ **Java tool port SAPJup (default port 6240)**
The Java tool port SAPJup is used for communication between SL Controller and the SAPJup Java program.

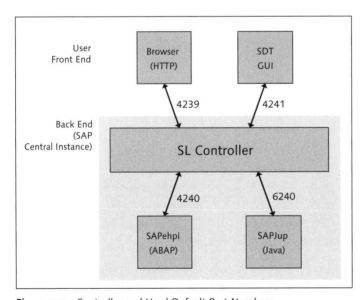

Figure 5.13 Controller and Used Default Port Numbers

Figure 5.13 illustrates the interaction between SL Controller and the other components. However, EHP Installer always uses the same default port numbers for the four ports listed previously. To implement multiple enhancement package installations on one physical host in parallel, you must change the default port numbers for each installation.

Table 5.2 shows a concept for assigning the ports: The basic idea is to prefix a consecutive number to each default port number (instead of changing them completely, which can become confusing quickly).

Port Types	Default Port Number	Ports for the First Installation	Ports for the Second Installation	Ports for the nth Installation
HTTP Port	4239	14239	24239	n4239
GUI Port	4241	14241	24241	n4241
ABAP Tool Port	4240	14240	24240	n4240
Java Tool Port	6240	16240	26240	n6240

Table 5.2 Concept for Assigning Port Numbers

You can flexibly assign the port numbers when you start EHP Installer (see Chapter 4, Section 4.5.7, Starting EHP Installer). For a better comparison, and for the sake of completeness, we also list the start command that EHP Installer uses for the default port numbers:

```
/EHPI/STARTUP jce_policy_zip=<path to JCE Policy archive>
```

You can use the following start command to assign any port number (the start command must be entered in one line)

```
/EHPI/STARTUP httpport=<Port> guiport=<port>
-srvarg=/DSUService/abaptoolport=<port>
-srvarg=/DSUService/javatoolport=<port>
jce_policy_zip=<path JCE Policy archive>
```

According to our concept, the start command for the first enhancement package installation would be the following:

```
/EHPI/STARTUP httpport=14239 guiport=14241
-srvarg=/DSUService/abaptoolport=14240
-srvarg=/DSUService/javatoolport=16240
jce_policy_zip=<path JCE Policy archive>
```

Before you start the installation you must therefore ensure that the port numbers are available. Also note that you can only implement multiple (parallel) enhancement package installations on pure ABAP-stack systems (this concept doesn't currently support dual-stack systems or Java systems). For more information, see SAP Note 1245473.

Shared <DIR_TRANS> Directory

Note that authorization problems can occur in the extraction of the SAR archives (support packages and enhancement packages) if you use a shared <DIR_TRANS> directory in which you implement enhancement package installations in parallel. The SAPCAR program checks the *ownership* of the packages and aborts if they are assigned to another user. You can avoid this problem by not storing the SAR archives of the support packages and enhancement packages in the download directory, but extracting them manually and copying them to the *Electronic Parcel Service inbox* (EPS inbox) of the transport directory (/SAPMNT/TRANS/EPS/IN). During the BIND_PATCH phase, EHP Installer reads the EPS inbox and adds all suitable support packages and enhancement packages to the installation queue. (Caution: This also applies to support packages that are not contained in the stack XML file!) Therefore, pay particular attention to which support package versions you integrate in the installation and remove them if necessary.

> **Recommendation**
>
> Empty the EPS inbox of the transport directory before you start an enhancement package installation. If this isn't possible, take note of the following: In the enhancement package _INCLUSION phase, EHP Installer initially determines the packages that are listed in the stack XML file. If you want to include additional support packages — for instance, support packages for your add-on software or the latest support packages for SAP HR — answer the user frontend question in the BIND_PATCH phase ("Do you want to include (further) Support Packages of the target release?") with YES.
>
> EHP Installer then reads the complete EPS inbox in a second step and adds all "suitable" support packages to its installation queue. In any case, carefully check which additional packages are offered for the integration in the installation! To do this, choose SHOW SELECTION in the following dialog to answer, "Do you want to take over the calculated package levels as default selection?" Only then can you check the actual found packages in detail and remove incorrect or superfluous support packages from the installation queue, if required.

Canceling the Enhancement Package Installation for the Startup Process in Virtual Environments

In the *Initialization* roadmap step (shortly after the EHP Installer startup), SL Controller searches for existing ABAP and Java instances. SL Controller searches for the following SAP instance profile name:

```
<SID>_DVEBMGS<SYSNR>_<PHYSICAL_HOSTNAME>
```

In virtual system environments, the SAP instance profile name is

```
<SID>_DVEBMGS<SYSNR>_<VIRTUAL_HOSTNAME>
```

The startup process ends with the following error message: "Error while creating request list — see proceeding messages. Unable to detect an ABAP and/or AS Java instance of the SAP system <SID> installed on host kamel."

This SL Controller error had not been remedied at the time this book was printed. Until it is, the problem can be resolved using a symbolic link in the profile directory. Proceed as follows to create a symbolic link (for Unix operating systems) in the profile directory from the SAP instance profile with the physical host name to the instance profile with the virtual host name:

```
ln -s <profile of the physical host name> <profile of the virtual
host name>
```

5.2.4   Configuring EHP Installer (Preconfigured Modes)

To parameterize the installation, EHP Installer provides *preconfigured modes* that you can select in the INITSUBST installation phase. These modes are predefined values that are used for an installation; for example, the number of background processes during downtime. If you decide on one of the preconfigured modes, you can take the predefined parameter values from the UPGCONFIG.XML file. This file is available in the installation directory under EHPI/ABAP/BIN. The expert option, MANUAL SELECTION OF PARAMETERS, is available in addition to selecting a mode. You should use this option if you have extensive knowledge of EHP Installer or need a customized parameterization of the tool. The option to manually set the parameters lets you adapt the installation specifically to your hardware environment and your requirements. You can also influence the following parameters when you select MANUAL SELECTION OF PARAMETERS:

- **Settings for generating invalidated loads with the following options:**

  - DO NOT START SGEN DURING THE UPGRADE.

  - FILL TABLE GENSETC WITH RELEVANT LOADS, BUT DO NOT RUN SGEN.

  - FILL TABLE GENSETC AND RUN SGEN WITH LOW RESOURCE CONSUMPTION.

  - FILL TABLE GENSETC AND RUN SGEN WITH HIGH RESOURCE CONSUMPTION.

  The GENSETC table contains the invalidated loads, which are generated by starting Transaction SGEN. Option 2 (FILL TABLE GENSETC WITH RELEVANT LOADS, BUT DO NOT RUN SGEN) means that the GENSETC table is filled with the invalidated loads and that the exact start time can still be determined manually. Options 3 and 4 (FILL TABLE GENSETC AND RUN SGEN WITH LOW/HIGH RESOURCE CONSUMPTION) start Transaction SGEN during the last phases of the enhancement package installation. The optimal setting depends on the time window of Transaction SGEN in your cutover planning, and on the duration of the SGEN execution.

  Experience has shown that customers often prefer a manual scheduling of Transaction SGEN and align the start time and the number of parallel processes with the further parallel activities of the go-live. For example, generating the invalid loads can lead to conflicts if transports are imported into the system in parallel, or transaction terminations can occur if the system is tested by the users.

- **Settings for database archiving with the following options:**

  - NO DISABLING OF THE ARCHIVE MODE (ARCHIVING ON)

  - THE ARCHIVE MODE SHOULD BE DISABLED IN PHASE STOPSAP_TRANS

  This selection basically depends on your backup strategy. As long as the archive mode is switched off, you can only recover the system for the last point in time of the last consistent database backup. If the database remains in the ARCHIVING ON mode during and after the technical downtime, you can also recover the database for a later point in time after the technical downtime (*rollforward recovery*, the recovery of the database state at a specific point in time with additional use of log files). This flexibility lets you align the next consistent database backup with the remaining activities of your cutover planning. You must consider the set of database logs that occurs during the technical downtime (their number is infinitesimal in relation to the generated database logs during the installation uptime). Ensure that sufficient space is available in the archive directory to avoid an "overflow" (*archiver stuck*) during downtime.

- **Configuration of parallel processes with the following options:**

  - ENTER THE HOST NAME OF YOUR BATCH SERVER (BATCH HOST)

  - ENTER THE MAXIMUM NUMBER OF BATCH PROCESSES DURING THE UPGRADE (BATCH PROCESSES)

  - ENTER THE MAXIMUM NUMBER OF PARALLEL PROCESSES DURING UPTIME (MAXIMUM UPTIME PROCESSES)

  - ENTER THE NUMBER OF PARALLEL IMPORT PROCESSES DURING DOWNTIME (R3TRANS PROCESSES)

  - TO OPTIMIZE MEMORY USAGE DURING ACTIVATION, YOU CAN USE THE SO-CALLED "MEMORY-OPTIMIZED ACTIVATOR." DO YOU WANT TO USE IT?

  In this dialog screen, you can specify the number of processes individually and thus influence the runtime of the installation to a certain degree. A general recommendation for the optimal values for setting the processes is not possible because the available hardware resources (CPU and main memory) significantly influence the parameterization. Another important influencing factor is the type of system (development, quality assurance, or production system) in which the enhancement package installation is carried out, and further customer-specific influencing factors. You can find additional information on setting the parameters in the *Troubleshooting and Administration Guide* of EHP Installer (available in your installation directory under EHPI/ABAP/HTDOC after the extraction of the SAR archive of EHP Installer). Section 5.3, Analysis and Optimization of an Enhancement Package Installation, provides further tips on how you can influence the installation runtime by setting these values.

- **Parameters for configuring the shadow instance**

  - YOU HAVE THE OPTION OF RUNNING THE SHADOW INSTANCE ON A DIFFERENT HOST IN YOUR SYSTEM LANDSCAPE. DO YOU WANT TO USE THIS OPTION?

  The shadow instance is always installed in the SAP central instance by default and operated in parallel to the live instance. In this dialog screen, you have the option of installing the shadow instance in another system. You can use this option if no free hardware resources are available in the SAP central instance.

5.2.5 Handling Add-ons in Enhancement Package Installations

A large set of add-ons is available to supplement a standard SAP system. Add-ons are programs that are imported into the SAP system via transports or the SAP Add-On Installation Tool (SAINT; they can contain customer-specific development objects, industry solutions, or plug-ins. We distinguish between two types of add-ons:

▶ SAP add-ons (products provided by SAP)

▶ Non-SAP add-ons (products provided by SAP partners or third parties)

The *add-on handling* — that is, the handling of add-on products for your SAP system — is an essential part of your enhancement package installation. In roadmap step 3, *Configuration*, in the IS_SELECT phase, you must decide how you want to proceed with the installed add-on products (see Roadmap Step 3: Configuration in Chapter 4, Section 4.5.10, Roadmap Steps of an Enhancement Package Installation). Usually, you have the following options:

▶ UPGRADE WITH ADD-ON CD

▶ UPGRADE WITH SAINT PACKAGE

▶ KEEP (WITH VENDOR KEY)

To decide on the appropriate procedure, we recommend that you identify the add-ons of your SAP system some time before the enhancement package installation. To do this, log on to your SAP system, and follow the SYSTEM • STATUS menu path. You can also view the entries in the CVERS table using Transaction SE16 (we prefer this alternative because the table contents are displayed more clearly). SAP Note 1226284 provides an overview of the SAP add-ons released for enhancement package 4.

The *vendor keys* of numerous non-SAP add-ons, which are released for enhancement package 4, are available in SAP Note 1262124. Comparable SAP notes will be created for future enhancement package versions. If your add-on is a third-party product, please contact your vendor directly. You must clarify the following points:

▶ Is the add-on product released for the enhancement package version you want to install?

▶ What is the exact procedure during the installation (that is, can you keep the current add-on version or do you need to implement an upgrade to a current version)?

▶ In the case of an add-on upgrade: Where do you find the update or SAINT package?

▶ If you keep the current version: Do you require a vendor key and what is the vendor key?

In addition to checking the installed add-ons, which you find in the CVERS table, you must also check to see if you've imported add-on products via transports into your SAP system. Some vendors deliver transports that customers must implement via the transport management system. Usually, these objects are assigned to a specific namespace. In such a case it is also recommended to contact the respective add-on provider. Clarify whether the proper functioning of the add-on is ensured after the enhancement package installation.

5.2.6 Important Commands for the Administration of the Shadow Instance

In Chapter 4, Section 4.5, SAP Enhancement Package Installer, you learned that a shadow instance is created within the enhancement package installation using EHP Installer. This shadow instance runs parallel to your live instance while you implement the modification adjustment (Transaction SPDD) and then start the activation. The last activity in the shadow instance is the removal of the activation errors.

There are situations in which you need to intervene in the installation routine. This section lists the commands for starting, stopping, locking, and unlocking the shadow instance:

▶ **Starting the shadow instance**
Go to the installation directory, /EHPI/ABAP/BIN. Use the ./SAPehpi startshd command to start the shadow instance.

▶ **Stopping the shadow instance**
Go to the installation directory, /EHPI/ABAP/BIN. Use the ./SAPehpi stopshd command to stop the shadow instance. Note that the shadow instance only runs between the phases, STARTSHDI_FIRST and STOPSHDI_LAST. Logging on to the shadow instance is only for modification adjustments and removing activation errors.

▶ **Unlocking the shadow instance**
A manual unlocking of the shadow instance can be required for removing activation errors. Call the following command:

```
cd EHPI/abap/bin
./SAPehpi unlockshd <SAPSID>
```

► **Locking the shadow instance**

Manually locking the shadow instance is imperative after a manual unlocking before you continue the installation routine. Call the following command:

```
cd EHPI/abap/bin
./SAPehpi lockshd <SAPSID>
```

► **Unlocking the system and the development environment**

In exceptional cases (for example, a support case) you must unlock the instance and undo a transport lock, if required. To do this, call the following commands:

```
tp unlocksys <SAPSID> pf=<path to transport profile>/tpprofile
tp unlock_eu <SAPSID> pf=<path to transport profile>/tpprofile
```

Use these commands only if the support team explicitly requests you do so. The unauthorized import of transports after an official locking of the development environment by EHP Installer means that you can bring your system to an inconsistent state; in the worst case, you may lose your support claims.

► **Locking the system and the development environment**

Always lock your system again before you continue the installation routine using the following commands:

```
tp locksys <SAPSID> pf=<path to transport profile>/tpprofile
tp lock_eu <SAPSID> pf=<path to transport profile>/tpprofile
```

5.2.7   Activation Errors in the ACT_UPG Phase

This chapter is supposed to provide some practical tips on analyzing the activation errors of the ACT_UPG phase. After you've adjusted the custom modifications in Transaction SPDD on the shadow system, start activating customer and SAP objects via the installation interface. The activation errors are displayed in the ACTUPG. ELG log file after the first installation run. You can find the log file in your installation directory under EHPI/ABAP/LOG. Open the log file and scroll through every single page. Caution: The error codes (return codes) are automatically set to value 8 for all transport requests as soon as one single error has occurred. The following is a brief excerpt of the ACTUPG.ELG log file:

```
****************************************************
*******   LIST OF ERRORS AND RETURN CODES   *******
****************************************************
~~~~~~~~~~~~~~~~~~~~~~~~~~~~~~~~~~~~~~~~~~~~~~~~~~~~~~
DDIC ACTIVATION ERRORS and RETURN CODE in SAPA-60012INFICA.SE1
```

```
~~~~~~~~~~~~~~~~~~~~~~~~~~~~~~~~~~~~~~~~~~~~~~~~~~~~~~~~~~~~~~~~~
1 ETP111 exit code           : "8"
~~~~~~~~~~~~~~~~~~~~~~~~~~~~~~~~~~~~~~~~~~~~~~~~~~~~~~~~~~~~~~~~~
DDIC ACTIVATION ERRORS and RETURN CODE in SAPA-60012INFICAX.SE1
~~~~~~~~~~~~~~~~~~~~~~~~~~~~~~~~~~~~~~~~~~~~~~~~~~~~~~~~~~~~~~~~~
1 ETP111 exit code           : "8"
```

As soon as you've identified the position in the log file that lists the exact activation error, you can start the error analysis. This example shows activation errors of the ACT_UPG phase of an enhancement package 4 installation:

```
~~~~~~~~~~~~~~~~~~~~~~~~~~~~~~~~~~~~~~~~~~~~~~~~~~~~~~~~~~~~~~~~~
DDIC ACTIVATION ERRORS and RETURN CODE in SAPAAAA701.DEV
~~~~~~~~~~~~~~~~~~~~~~~~~~~~~~~~~~~~~~~~~~~~~~~~~~~~~~~~~~~~~~~~~
1EEDO536 "Technical Settings" "USMDZ60020C" could not be activated
1EEDO536 "Technical Settings" "USMDZ6201C" could not be activated
1EEDO519 "Srch Help" "H_5ITCN" could not be activated
1EEDO519 "Srch Help" "H_5ITTT" could not be activated
1EEDO536 "Table" "ZINFO_ZAHLUNG" could not be activated
1 ETP111 exit code           : "8"
```

You can obtain the following information from this error text:

▶ The SAPAAAA701.DEV activation log contains additional information on the exact error cause.

▶ Tables, technical settings, and search helps could not be activated.

In the next step, analyze the exact error cause in the activation log; in this example, the SAPAAAA701.DEV log. Bear in mind during this analysis that multiple activation errors can have the same cause; for example, if a dependent object could not be activated. This means that if a structure could not be activated, the programs that use this structure cannot be activated either.

You can also remedy errors by simply repeating the activation phase; for example, if objects were activated in the wrong sequence in the first activation run. In the case of activation errors of SAP objects, check to see if a corresponding SAP Note is available in the SAP Service Marketplace. SAP Note 1143022 includes a section on which activation errors occur most frequently during the enhancement package 4 import, and how these can be solved.

You can remedy activation errors directly in the shadow instance you've previously unlocked. To do this, call the corresponding object in Transaction SE11, and eliminate the cause.

An incorrect or incomplete SPDD adjustment can also be a cause for the activation error. By no means should you ignore activation errors of tables containing data, because this can lead to data loss or, in the worst case, follow-up errors in the installation procedure. Do not continue with the installation until you've removed all critical activation errors, unless they are errors that can be ignored (this is documented in SAP Notes 1143022 and 1243014 for SAP objects, for example).

5.2.8 Important Checkpoints before Starting the Technical Downtime

Before you start the technical downtime of an enhancement package installation in roadmap step 6 (*Downtime*), you must implement a couple of manual checks. Only when these checks and preparations on the system side are completed successfully can you securely transfer your system to downtime. These checks primarily ensure the consistency of your SAP system. A complete list of manual checkpoints is customer-specific and should be included in the cutover planning point by point. This section is supposed to provide some generic checkpoints that you can then supplement with your own checkpoints (see Table 5.3).

Functional Preparations	
1.1	List of SAP users that must log on to the SAP system after the technical downtime (for example, to start the transports or for functional tests of the system) is created.
1.2	All "functional," that is, business-critical, background jobs are complete (payment runs, job chains, and so on) and planned.
1.3	Outstanding updates are processed.
1.4	Canceled updates are deleted (Transaction SM13).
1.5	...
IT Infrastructure and Database-specific Preparations	
2.1	Deactivation of the cluster failover during the technical downtime.
2.2	Free memory space available in the database?
2.3	Required memory space available in the file systems?
2.4	Automatic restart of the SAP system deactivated?
2.5	Database statistics updated (if necessary)?
2.6	...

Table 5.3 Manual Checks before Starting Technical Downtime

Functional Preparations

Preparations on the SAP System Side

3.1 Setting a system message (Transaction SM02) with the information that the production system is not available.

3.2 No SAP object locked by repairs.

3.3 Consistency check (missing tables and indexes) successful (Transaction DB02).

3.4 Background jobs of the job class C configured for central instance.

3.5 RDDIMPDP background job configured on central instance.

3.6 Batch processes configured on the SAP central instance.

3.7 Locking of SAP users.

3.8 No active user logged on to system.

3.9 No open or aborted update in the system (Transaction SM13).

3.10 BW delta queues processed.

3.11 General: interface queues cleaned.

3.12 Monitoring tools (application server and central instance) stopped during downtime.

3.13 Isolation of central instance (stopping the application servers).

3.14 Consistent database backup exists, including the last database logs (online or offline backup).

3.15 Consistent backup of the installation directory, of kernel directory, and SAP profiles available.

3.16 ...

Table 5.3 Manual Checks before Starting Technical Downtime (Cont.)

Practical Tip

The RSINDCRE batch job is scheduled during roadmap step 5 (*Preprocessing*) in the RUNASYN_RSINDCRE phase. This batch job tries to create all secondary indexes that can already be created during uptime. If the creation of an index fails, it is repeated during the technical downtime in the PARCONV_UPG phase. In exceptional cases, this can mean that the downtime is longer than in previous test runs. Therefore, several hours before you start the technical downtime, you must check the following:

> ▶ After the RUNASYN_RSINDCRE phase, you can use Transaction SM37 to check whether the RSINDCRE batch job was completed.
>
> ▶ In the RSINDCRE.<SID> log file in the EHPI/ABAP/LOG/ directory, you must check to see if all secondary indexes were created successfully. If required, you can compare the content with the corresponding log from the previous test run.

If these and additional checks are processed successfully, a formal release for the technical downtime can occur, and the administrator can continue with the installation. During the technical downtime, you can perform monitoring on the operating system and SAP side; for example, you can monitor the processor and memory utilization in the SAP central instance and database instance.

Practical Tip

In the cutover planning, determine various milestones of the technical downtime with precise specifications when an installation phase must be complete or when an installation phase begins (this information is available from the enhancement package installation of your QAS system). The following phases, which are carried out during the technical downtime, are particularly suited as milestones:

▶ PARCONV_UPG

▶ TABIM_UPG

▶ TABIM_POST

▶ XPRAS_UPG

With these time specifications during the downtime of the production system, you can determine whether individual phases have a longer or a shorter runtime. Moreover, you keep an overview of whether you can meet the calculated timeframe of the technical downtime, or whether there are delays.

5.2.9 Generating a Print Revision of an Enhancement Package Installation

The print revision is an installation-specific phase list that includes all phases and their precise runtimes. This information can be very helpful if, for example, you want to create a detailed schedule of the installation in production. Using a workaround, you can generate a detailed phase list from the runtime analysis (UPGANA. XML). This list includes all phases that were executed in your installation. Proceed as follows:

1. Copy the UPGANA.XML and UPGANALYSIS.XLS files to a local directory after a completed installation. You can find these two files in your installation directory under /EHPI/ABAP/ HTDOC/EVAL.

   The UPGANA.XML file is the runtime analysis, and the UPGANALYSIS.XLS file is the associated XML style sheet, which converts the runtime analysis into a readable HTML format.

2. Open the UPGANALYSIS.XML style sheet in WordPad or a comparable tool. In the header area of the file you can find the following line:

   ```
   <xsl:param name="cutofftime">30</xsl:param>
   ```

3. Now change the value of the cut-off time from 30 to 00. The changed line now looks as follows:

   ```
   <xsl:param name="cutofftime">00</xsl:param>
   ```

   Save your changes (see Figure 5.14).

```
<?xml version="1.0" encoding="UTF-8" ?>
<!--    ************************************************* -->
<!--    Transforms UPGANA.XML as generated by the UPGEVAL -->
<!--     phases into a human readable HTML format          -->
<!--          Copyright 2006-2008 SAP-AG                   -->
<!--    ************************************************* -->

<!-- $Id: //bc_control/LM-SL/702_COR/ehpi/HTDOC/htdoc/UpgAnalysis.xsl#4 $  -->

<xsl:stylesheet version="1.0" xmlns:xsl="http://www.w3.org/1999/XSL/Transform">
  <xsl:param name="title"/>
  <xsl:param name="creationdate"/>
  <xsl:param name="contact"/>
  <xsl:param name="cutofftime">30</xsl:param>
```

Figure 5.14 Excerpt of the "UpgAnalysis.xls" Style Sheet

Double-click to open the runtime analysis file, UPGANA.XML, with the changed style sheet. In the medium area of the runtime analysis, you can now find a list of all installation phases, including a precise specification of the runtime. You can also change the value of the cut-off time to a higher value — for instance, to 60 — only if phases are supposed to be listed that ran for at least 60 seconds or longer. Installation phases in which a dialog input (or an error dialog) occurred are always displayed independent of the runtime.

5.2.10 Maintenance Project after Completion of an Enhancement Package Installation

In principle, SAP provides support packages for each software component, regardless of the version of the respective component. This means that there are support packages for software components of versions 600, 602, 603, 604, and so on. An SAP ERP 6.0 enhancement package 4 system contains a combination of application-related software components in versions 600 and 604. These different versions also require different support packages (see SAP Note 1297231):

▶ Software components of version 600 require SAP ERP 6.0 support packages.

▶ Software components of version 604 require the equivalent enhancement package 4 support packages.

Make sure that the support packages are calculated and downloaded for future maintenance projects via a maintenance transaction, and that the system data is up to date in the SAP Solution Manager system landscape. The Maintenance Optimizer automatically calculates the support packages required for the various software components; you can then import these support packages into your SAP ERP 6.0 system using Transaction SPAM, as usual. There are no major changes for a maintenance project after an enhancement package installation.

> **Note**
>
> SAP provides a delivery calendar for support package stacks. From this calendar you can learn the *anticipated* delivery dates of support package stacks of a calendar year. This information is very helpful for planning maintenance projects. You can find the delivery calendar for support package stacks at *http://service.sap.com/sp-stacks* • SP STACK SCHEDULE.

5.3 Analysis and Optimization of an Enhancement Package Installation

The runtime of an enhancement package installation with EHP Installer does not always meet the requirements of some customers. The possible causes for a long installation runtime are varied, so a statement about the cause is not possible without a profound analysis. This section first discusses some planning-relevant terms and describes them based on graphics. This is followed by influencing factors and current customer statistics.

5.3.1 Comparing Uptime, Downtime, and Business Downtime

An enhancement package installation can be divided into two logical subareas: uptime and technical downtime. The uptime comprises the roadmap steps 1 through 5 of EHP Installer, in which the SAP system is used in production. The technical downtime comprises roadmap step 6, in which the SAP system is locked for user logins. Theoretically, roadmap steps 7 and 8 are no longer part of the technical downtime, because the SAP system is already unlocked here; in practical use, however, the manual technical postprocessing for the system often starts when the installation tool is finished after the *Finalization* roadmap step. Figure 5.15 compares the uptime and the technical downtime based on the roadmap steps of EHP Installer.

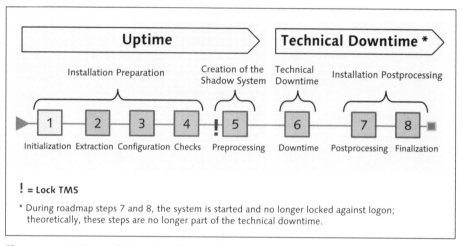

Figure 5.15 Uptime and Downtime Phases of EHP Installer

The technical downtime is encapsulated by the business downtime. Figure 5.16 shows the different perspectives of an enhancement package implementation from the user view (*business perspective*) and the technical view (*technical perspective*).

5.3.2 Installation Runtime and Downtime

Many factors can influence the runtime and downtime of an enhancement package installation. These can be divided into three classes:

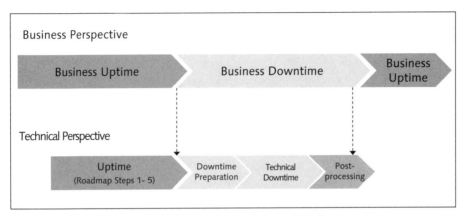

Figure 5.16 Comparing the Business Perspective and the Technical Perspective

- **Hardware**
  - Number of processors and processor performance of the database server and the application server
  - Memory; that is, available physical main memory
  - Capacity of the hard disk subsystem (input/output processing of the hard disks)
- **Software**
  - Product version of the start release SAP ERP 6.0 and the target product version; for example, SAP ERP 6.0 enhancement package 3 to SAP ERP 6.0 enhancement package 4
  - Version of the installation tool, EHP Installer
  - Versions of the `tp` and `R3trans` programs
- **Configuration**
  - Parameterization of EHP Installer (for example, number of parallel processes)
  - Parameterization of the SAP ERP system, the shadow instance (instance profile), and the database
  - Number of customer-specific clients
  - Number of installed languages

- ▶ Number and type of the selected technical usages
- ▶ Number of support packages that are part of the installation queue and the additionally integrated support packages
- ▶ Usage of the incremental table implementation (Transaction ICNV)

> **Note**
>
> Database size usually has no influence on the installation runtime or the downtime (except when converting large customer-specific tables during downtime).

Figure 5.17 shows statistical evaluations of test and production systems of customers based on their runtime analysis files (UPGANA.XML).

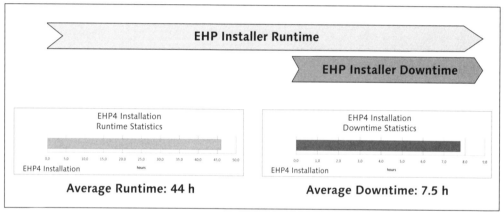

Figure 5.17 Runtime Statistics of EHP Installer for Enhancement Package 4 for SAP ERP (Based on 383 Evaluated Files, December 2009)

5.3.3 Runtime Analysis File of an Enhancement Package Installation

Shortly before completing an enhancement package installation in the CREATE_ UPGEVAL phase, EHP Installer generates a runtime analysis file in XML format, which is stored as UPGANA.XML in the installation directory under /EHPI/ABAP/ HTDOC/EVAL (see Figure 5.18). Copy this runtime analysis file and the UPGANALYSIS. XSL style sheet to your local directory on your PC.

SAP Enhancement Package Installer ERP			
OPEN ALL CLOSE ALL	>>Components	>>PREPARE	>>MAIN
>>XPRAS	>>AFTER-IMPORT-METHODS	>>CONVERSIONS	>>DDLs
>>TRANSPORTS	>>Process statistics		
−System			
Start-Release:	700	Destination-Release:	700
SID:	ERP	Installation number:	0020221773
DB-Type:	ORACLE	OS-Type:	AIX
DB-Version:	10.2.0.2.0	OS-Version:	5.3.0
DB size (initial):	2768.47/2948.21 GB	SAP-Host:	saperp
DB size (final):	2709.51/3058.21 GB	DB-Host:	saperpdb
NR-Clients (productive):	2 (1)		
−Configuration			
Strategy:	Downtime-minimized	Archiving:	STOPSAP_TRANS
Batch processes:	8	Uptime processes:	8
R3trans processes:	8	R3load processes:	1
Imported Languages:			
J2EE present:	0		
+Times			
+Versions			
+Tool versions			
+Component versions			

Figure 5.18 Excerpt from the UPGANA.XML Runtime Analysis File

UPGANA.XML contains the most critical information on your enhancement package installation in a clear form and is therefore used to make a detailed analysis of the runtime and downtime. It also forms the entry point for a targeted identification of optimization potentials. The UPGANA.XML file is subdivided into multiple sections that you can expand or close by clicking on the OPEN ALL and CLOSE ALL BUTTONS IN THE HEADER area of the file (see Figure 5.18).

The following list describes the individual sections of the UPGANA.XML file in detail:

▸ **System section**
The SYSTEM section provides general information on the database and the operating system, and you can use it for initial orientation. Information, such as database size (net/gross), vendor and version of the database and operating system, and the number of clients, is presented in a clear format.

▸ **Configuration section**
Here, you learn which parameterization was used for the installation.

▸ **Times section**
The TIMES section includes start and end data, and exact specifications on the duration of the technical downtime (minimum downtime) and the overall

installation runtime. In the line SINCE START_SHDI_FIRST you can find the installation runtime of the START_SHDI_FIRST phase. This is the phase in which the shadow instance is started for the first time. The line SINCE DB_CLONE lists the installation runtime of the DB_CLONE phase. This specification is very important for your cutover planning, because EHP Installer blocks the development and transport environment shortly before this phase.

▶ **Versions and Tool Versions sections**
In these two areas, is a clear list of the tool versions used; for example, the version of EHP Installer and the versions of the `tp` transport control program and the `R3trans` program of the initial and the target environment.

▶ **Component Versions section**
This section lists all software components, software component versions, and support package versions of your system, including any installed add-on product components. The "REL" column name (Release) stands for the version of a software component and "PL" (Patch Level) for the support package version.

The values in the SOURCE column describe the initial status of a system, the EXPORT column refers to the shadow system, and the DESTINATION column to the target system.

The values in the SOURCE and EXPORT columns are identical in an enhancement package installation (because the shadow system is established from the source system). By comparing the SOURCE and DESTINATION columns, you can determine the integrated enhancement package components (the versions of the software components are different) and the integrated support package versions.

▶ **Sections for the steps for roadmap steps 2 through 7 of EHP Installer**
These sections provide a list of the roadmap steps of the enhancement package installation. In total, there are only six different steps; roadmap steps 1 and 8 (*Initialization* and *Finalization*) are steps of SL Controller and they last for only a few seconds; therefore, they are not listed separately here. A step, in turn, can be subdivided into various modules, which is primarily done for reasons of clarity. The information on the cut-off time behind the respective roadmap step indicates as of what duration phases are listed. A cut-off time with the value 30, for example, lists all phases with a duration of 30 seconds or higher. You can change this setting in the UPGANALYSIS.XSL style sheet. Section 5.2.9, Generating a Print Revision of an Enhancement Package Installation, provides instructions for this.

Open a roadmap step as an example. The detail view shows the phase name, the runtime (TIME column), how often the phase was run (RUNS column), and the number of errors per phase (FAILED column). Phases that contain one or more dialog inputs are indicated with + dialogs in the TIMES column. Phases indicated in red were canceled with an error dialog.

▶ **Downtime (Execute) section**
To perform an in-depth analysis of the technical downtime, you must consider the phase runtimes of the DOWNTIME or EXECUTE step in more detail. Identify all phases that stand out due to a long runtime (for example, a runtime > 1 hour). Section 5.3.2, Evaluating the Runtime Analysis File, provides more information on the analysis of the technical downtime.

▶ **XPRAS and After-Import Methods sections**
These two sections list reports that run in the XPRAS_UPG phase. It is worthwhile to take a closer look to identify potential "long runners."

▶ **Conversions section**
The CONVERSIONS area lists tables that are *converted* during the technical downtime; that is, the table is created with the new technical layout, and its contents are copied.

The table conversion takes place during the technical downtime in the PARCONV_UPG phase. It can lead to a considerable extension of the technical downtime, so it is an essential part of the downtime analysis to take a close look at this area.

▶ **DDLs section**
The DDLs section lists tables for SQL statements such as create index or alter table, which are triggered in the PARCONV_UPG or PARMVNT_XCNV downtime phases. Changing a table definition (for example, by adding a new field to a table) or creating a new index can be very time-consuming.

▶ **Transports section**
The TRANSPORTS section lists the transports that are imported into the database during the main import of the technical downtime (TABIM_UPG phase).

▶ **Process Statistics section**
This section lists the statistical evaluations on the percentage runtime of the individual transports, reports, or executable programs. These evaluations provide information about whether the selected number of parallel processes was sufficient or whether an additional parallelization offers more optimization potential.

> **Note**
>
> You can generate a "preliminary" runtime analysis file during a running installation. To do this, go to the installation directory under /EHPI/ABAP/BIN on your SAP central instance, and execute the following command:
>
> ```
> ./SAPehpi xmlanalysis <file name>.XML
> ```
>
> You can execute the command at any point in time during the installation and as often as you like. It creates a file in XML format in the /EHPI/ABAP/BIN directory. You can view this file using the UPGANALYSIS.XSL style sheet on your local computer in a readable HTTP format. With this "preliminary" runtime analysis file, you can obtain an overview of installation phases and runtimes executed up to this point before the enhancement package installation is complete.

5.3.4 Evaluating the Runtime Analysis File

Section 5.3.3 presented the structure of the UPGANA.XML file. Here, we explain how you can evaluate the runtime of the technical downtime, which is possible as soon as you've completed an enhancement package installation using EHP Installer and copied the UPGANA.XML file to your local PC.

You can find the duration of the technical downtime in the TIMES section in the MINIMUM DOWNTIME line. This information refers to the net runtime without the wait time of dialog inputs if terminations occurred during the technical downtime. Now go to the STEP: EXECUTE section. This section comprises the phases of the technical downtime. For your orientation: One of the first phases of technical downtime is the MODPROF_TRANS phase or the DOWNCONF_TRANS phase (depending on the settings of the cut-off time in the UPGANALYSIS.XSL file). Check the runtime of all phases listed here and write down the phases with the longest runtimes. Long-running phases usually include the following:

- ► PARCONV_UPG
- ► TABIM_UPG
- ► TABIM_POST
- ► XPRAS_UPG

Also analyze the phases of the *Postprocessing* roadmap step in the STEP: POST-EXECUTE section. Although these phases run after the technical downtime, they can postpone the start of the manual technical postprocessing on a transition weekend. A potential long-running phase is the JOB_RASUVAR2 phase (recovery of the program variants).

Then navigate to the XPRAS and AFTER-IMPORT METHODS sections to identify long-running reports. Long-running reports can include the following:

► ENHS_AFTER_IMPORT

► SUSR_AFTER_IMP_PROFILE

In the next section, CONVERSIONS, you determine whether a time-consuming table conversion occurred. All table conversions are listed here.

The next section, DDLs, informs you whether an expensive SQL statement, for example, `create index`, consumes valuable time. For detailed analyses, you must check the PD* log files in the installation directory under /EHPI/ABAP/LOG.

If you've analyzed the UPGANA.XML file according to this procedure, you know about the time-consuming phases and activities of your enhancement package installation. The following sections describe some optimization options.

5.3.5 General Recommendations on Optimizing the Downtime

The technical downtime is part of the business downtime. Besides the technical downtime, there is a whole series of additional activities that also considerably influence the entire business downtime. To analyze and optimize the technical downtime with minute precision, neither effort nor expenses are spared; but other activities — for example, a full backup or import of transports — can take several hours, which is considered normal. A holistic approach of a downtime optimization should not be limited to the optimization of individual phases of EHP Installer; rather it is necessary to challenge all system activities and processes. Only with such an advanced view is it possible to reduce the downtime of the production system to a minimum. This section presents some recommendations for optimizing the uptime, downtime, and manual work after the technical downtime.

General Recommendations

► Use the latest enhancement package installer tool. (Note: If you've used a tool version successfully, you should "freeze" this version and use it for implementing all other installations.)

► Use the current transport tools, `tp` and `R3trans`, on your source system and for the enhancement package installation.

► Delete unused clients.

▶ Install technical usages that you actually need (refer to Section 5.1.2, Practical Approach for Selecting Relevant Technical Usages).

▶ Do not install any "superfluous" support packages (see Section 5.1.6, Deselecting Packages of the Installation Queue).

▶ Create the installation directory directly on the SAP central instance (not as an NFS share or mapped directory).

▶ Update your database statistics before you start EHP Installer and update it again, if required, before the technical downtime (for Oracle databases, for example, see SAP Note 1232776). Also check the statistics for D* tables; for example, `D010INC` or `D010TAB` (SAP Note 1232776).

▶ Profile parameters: Check the values of the SAP instance profile based on the available SAP notes.

▶ Database parameters and patches: Check the parameter settings of your database based on the available SAP notes, and check the currently available patches for your database version; for example, SAP Notes 830576 and 1137346.

▶ Recovery of variants (JOB_RASUVAR2): In the case of a very long runtime of the JOB_RASUVAR2 phase, manually start the report for recovering the variants after the technical downtime (that is, in parallel to the other technical activities). For more information, refer to SAP Note 1052664.

5.3.6 Optimization Potential of Parallel Processes

This section describes parallel processes and the effects they have on an enhancement package installation. This information includes setting recommendations. There are three different setting options in EHP Installer: maximum uptime processes, batch processes, and R3trans processes.

Maximum Uptime Processes

The number of uptime processes determines the maximum number of background and R3trans processes that are used during the installation uptime (that is, while the system is used in production). Figure 5.19 illustrates this context based on two examples. You can see the effect of the selected uptime processes on the batch and R3trans processes that are used during the installation uptime and the installation downtime. Based on these examples you can see that the value of the uptime processes limits the other processes during uptime. Accordingly, by means of the number of uptime processes, you can influence the installation runtime *before* the technical downtime. A low value of uptime processes means that the uptime extends over a longer period of time, whereas little or no influence on the live operation is to be expected. A high value of uptime processes shortens the installation runtime before the technical downtime, whereas the influence on the live operation can increase.

Determine the duration of the uptime so that you know the latest start time of the enhancement package installation, and add one to three or more days as a buffer for this start time (for unexpected problems and the influence of the live operation on the installation runtime). In this planning, you also need to calculate the time at which the development environment is locked (REPACHK2 phase), because this must be communicated in good time.

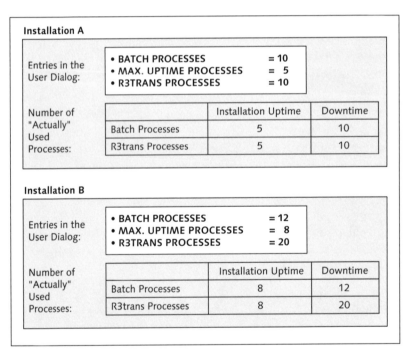

Installation A

Entries in the User Dialog:	• BATCH PROCESSES = 10 • MAX. UPTIME PROCESSES = 5 • R3TRANS PROCESSES = 10		

Number of "Actually" Used Processes:		Installation Uptime	Downtime
	Batch Processes	5	10
	R3trans Processes	5	10

Installation B

Entries in the User Dialog:	• BATCH PROCESSES = 12 • MAX. UPTIME PROCESSES = 8 • R3TRANS PROCESSES = 20		

Number of "Actually" Used Processes:		Installation Uptime	Downtime
	Batch Processes	8	12
	R3trans Processes	8	20

Figure 5.19 Effect of Uptime Processes Based on an Example

A concrete recommendation is not possible because many factors take effect here. You should use a moderate value of 4 to 8 uptime processes and test this value in advance in the QAS system.

Batch Processes

The number of batch processes determines the maximum number of background processes that are used for the activities of EHP Installer during the technical downtime. The following rule of thumb is used to calculate the optimal parameterization:

Batch processes = number of CPUs x 2

Note that values that are too high can have a negative effect on the downtime (database lock situation, among other things).

R3trans Processes

The number of R3trans processes determines how many parallel R3trans processes can be used to import data into the database (for example, during the main import in the TABIM_UPG downtime phase). The following rule of thumb is used to calculate the optimal parameterization:

512 MB of main memory for each R3trans process

Note that an improvement on the import speed can no longer be achieved to a specific value, because the level of parallelization is also limited by other factors (for example, package attributes, transport buffer).

Ideally, you should test the effects of the different parameter values on the installation runtime and downtime in a sandbox system, depending on how critical your downtime requirements are. *Always* test the parameter values you want to use for your installation in production on your QAS system first. Only then can you forecast the expected installation runtime and downtime (taking into account the different hardware capacities of the QAS and the PRD system).

5.3.7 Optimization Potential of Individual Downtime Phases

Table 5.4 contains information on the optimization potential of individual downtime phases of an enhancement package installation. Consult the referenced SAP notes for detailed instructions.

Phase	Details	Recommendation/Potential
PARCONV_UPG	Table conversion	Check to see if using of Transaction ICNV (Incremental Table Conversion) is possible. For more information, refer to the Troubleshooting and Administration Guide; see Section 5.2.1, Additional Documentation and Information.
TABIM_UPG	Main import during the technical downtime	Check the number of parallel processes and increase it if necessary.
TABIM_POST	Mass activation of enhancement spots	See SAP Notes 1369430, 1360490, and 1346046.
XPRAS_UPG	Execution of XPRAS and after-import methods. ▸ WEBI_AFTER_IMPORT ▸ ENHS_AFTER_IMPORT ▸ SUSR_AFTER_IMP_ PROFILE ▸ WEBI_AFTER_IMPORT	General: See SAP Note 1346046. ▸ See SAP Note 1232776. ▸ See SAP Note 1062559. ▸ See SAP Note 821496. ▸ See SAP Note 1279597.

Table 5.4 Downtime Phases and Optimization Potential

Recommendations on Optimizing Manual Postprocessing

You have two options if you want to improve manual postprocessing:

▸ **Integration of modification adjustment transports**
Integrate the transports with the enhancement package installation (ADJUST-PRP phase) using the modification adjustment (Transaction SPAU).

▸ **Integration of a correction transport**
You have the option of integrating a customer-specific correction transport (*single change request*) with the enhancement package installation in the BIND_ PATCH phase. When you integrate your bundled customer-specific correction transport with the enhancement package installation, it is imported in the TABIM_UPG downtime phase.

5.4   Recommendations on Activating Business Functions

If you want to install enhancement packages in your SAP ERP system and use new functions, which are provided via business functions, you must address the following question: When should the business functions be switched on? In principle, you have two options:

▶ Directly after the technical installation (that is, in a downtime window)

▶ At a later point in time

Switching on business functions must only be done when no end user is working in the SAP system and no background jobs are being run. This means that business downtime must be communicated and implemented for the activation period of a business function. You should carry out the following steps when you switch on business functions, regardless of when the activation takes place.

5.4.1   Preparations

Take care of the following when preparing the switch on:

▶ Check the documentation and release notes of the business function in advance.

▶ Use the documentations provided by SAP to check which customizing settings and adaptations are required after switching on a dedicated business function, so that the new business function can be used in production.

▶ Examine the test catalog of the respective business function, and complete your test cases.

▶ Check to see if end-user training is required, and plan appropriately.

▶ Optional: Test the activation of a business function in a sandbox system. (Note: Up to enhancement package 4 for SAP ERP 6.0, you can't switch off a business function.)

5.4.2   Switching On a Business Function

To switch on a business function in your SAP system, go to Transaction SFW5.

1. **Select the business function**
   Open the ENTERPRISE_BUSINESS_FUNCTIONS folder, and navigate to the business function you want to switch on. You can switch on several business

functions at the same time in one activation process (recommended). Industry-specific business functions become visible in Transaction SFW5 after you've selected the appropriate industry using the BUSINESS FUNCTION SET checkbox.

2. **Check dependencies (consistency check)**
   In the PLANNED STATE column, use the respective checkboxes of the business functions that you want to switch on. Now click on the CHECK CHANGES button. Using this function you only check the functional interdependencies of the business functions. There is no activation yet.

3. **Eliminate inconsistencies**
   The system opens a new dialog window showing the results of the consistency check for each business function. Two results are possible:

   ▶ No inconsistencies exist: You can switch your selected business functions on in the next step.

   ▶ Inconsistencies exist: Before you can switch your business functions on, you must first eliminate the conflicts mentioned. For example, a typical conflict is that the switching on of a business function requires another business function or enterprise extension (message text: "Business Function xx is prerequisite for Business Function xy"). The dialog window shows details on the conflict that occurred. Eliminate this conflict, and restart the check.

4. **Switch on the business function**
   If the check is without any errors, you can start the activation process of your business functions using the ACTIVATE CHANGES button (see Chapter 2, Architecture and Technology). This process schedules the SFW_ACTIVATE_SFOX background job. This background job activates the switch settings, that is, the functional enhancements are switched on; as a result, changes in the menu and the user interfaces become visible, for example. Write down the *exact runtime* of the background job. This information will help you plan the required business downtime of the production system. You can restart a terminated activation run by following the SYSTEM SETTINGS • ACTIVATE RESTART menu path.

5. **Control activation log (optional)**
   You receive an activation log after the activation. You can call all activation logs at any time via the GOTO • SWITCH FRAMEWORK • LOGS menu path. The activation logs show which objects are affected by the activation and were adapted; for example, which switch BC sets were extracted. In the DDIC LOGS menu options, only the DDIC part of the activation is shown if the DDIC was affected

by the activation. Switched on business functions and enterprise extensions are indicated with a yellow bulb.

6. **Create transport request**

Now create a transport request via the SYSTEM SETTINGS • TRANSPORT menu path, which includes the switch on process (the switch setting). We recommend that you import the activation in the downstream systems (QAS and PRD) not manually, but via a transport request. The business functions are then automatically switched on during the transport import.

Practical Tip

If you transport the activation of a business function to downstream systems, all switch settings are always transferred.

Example:

You switch on business functions A and B, but don't create a transport request for them. On the following day, you switch on business functions C, D, and E and then create a transport request. This transport request includes all active switch settings of this system. If you then transport this transport request to a downstream system, the business functions A, B, C, D, and E are switched on.

If you want to switch on a subset of the business functions that are switched on in the development system in the downstream systems, you must activate them manually in the development system and in all downstream systems. If business functions are switched on in a system, this is always a cross-client setting. See Chapter 2, Section 2.4.3, Transport of Switch Statuses in System Landscapes.

---

7. **Adaptations and customizing settings**

After you've activated the business functions in your system, customizing settings and other functional adaptations may be necessary. You can find information on this topic in the documentations and release notes of the respective business function.

8. **Test**

Use the test catalogs and test case templates to start your individual system and acceptance tests. The delivered test case templates include examples that show you how to test the new business functions. You can also adapt and enhance these templates. You can find instructions on working with test case templates in the SAP online help at *http://help.sap.com* • SAP ERP CENTRAL COMPONENT • SAP ERP ENHANCEMENT PACKAGES • BUSINESS FUNCTIONS (SAP ENHANCEMENT PACKAGE 4 FOR SAP ERP 6.0) • INTRODUCTION: ENHANCEMENT PACKAGES AND BUSINESS FUNCTIONS • WORKING WITH TEST CASE TEMPLATES.

The Authors

Martina Kaplan has been working as a senior consultant in technical consulting at SAP Deutschland AG & Co. KG since 2006. Prior to that, she worked as a technical consultant at CSC Ploenzke AG in Wiesbaden, Germany, where she developed her skills in SAP technology and upgrades.

Her current work focuses on enhancement packages, upgrades, and upgrade project management. Since 2008, she has led the upgrade focus group and managed many national and international customer projects from planning to implementation. Besides her project work, Martina is also responsible for further service development in these areas. You can contact her at *martina.kaplan@sap.com*.

Christian Oehler joined SAP in 1999. He has been working as a solution manager at SAP AG since 2007. His areas of responsibility within the SAP Business Suite include Application Lifecycle Management and TCO, where enhancement packages have been a main focus for many years. Previously, he worked as a senior technical consultant at SAP Deutschland AG & Co. KG. There he was responsible for the upgrade focus group. Furthermore, Christian managed many national and international customer projects from planning to implementation.

Christian Oehler studied at the Baden-Wuerttemberg Cooperative State University in Karlsruhe, Germany and holds a Bachelor of Science in Information Technology. He is currently studying for his MBA at the Open University Business School, Milton Keynes (UK). You can contact him at *christian.oehler@sap.com*.

Torsten Kamenz is an SAP Business Suite development architect at SAP AG. His work focuses on the architecture for SAP enhancement packages and on the implementation in development guidelines for SAP Business Suite product development. Previously, he spent several years working on product development for SAP Human Resources Management, where he was responsible for development projects for self-services and performance management. He then worked on the Business Suite Core Architecture, where he developed application frameworks in AS Java and SAP NetWeaver Portal. Since 2006, he and Andreas Kemmler have been responsible for implementing the enhancement package strategy in SAP Business Suite product development.

Andreas Kemmler joined SAP AG in 1997 and has held various positions in product development since then. He started in Human Resources Management development, where he was responsible for several development projects and application frameworks. He then moved to ERP architecture, and later to the core architecture of SAP Business Suite, where he assumed co-responsibility for implementing Service-Oriented Architecture (SOA). In 2006, he and Torsten Kamenz were entrusted with the task of developing a programming model that could be used to implement and provide comprehensive switchable enhancements and further developments in the SAP ERP system, which became the basis for enhancement packages. The resulting guidelines were then extended to the entire enhancement package development of SAP Business Suite. Since then, Andreas Kemmler and Torsten Kamenz have been responsible for the development guidelines for enhancement package development for SAP Business Suite. Since 2007, he has worked as a program architect for ERP enhancement packages.

Frank Zweissig joined SAP in 1993. Previously, he worked for the Oil & Gas industry solution as a developer, architect, and project lead for seven years, particularly in bulk material transport. He then moved to the high-tech industry business unit as the manager of the solution development team. Subsequently, he became the project lead for manufacturing industries development and later the program lead for integrating industry solutions with the standard SAP ERP solution. He was part of the team that developed the Switch Framework and the enhancement package concept. Today, he is a delivery manager for Industries & Asset development, where he is responsible for the projects in this area.

Index

Develop a custom monitoring concept with all objects and attributes

Many screenshots and instructions help you to follow the implementation step by step

Up-to-date for SAP Solution Manager, enterprise edition

Corina Weidmann, Lars Teuber

Conception and Installation of System Monitoring Using the SAP Solution

SAP PRESS Essentials 74

This detailed guide is an essential book for administrators looking to develop and implement a custom monitoring concept in SAP Solution Manager. Using step by step instructions, and updated for SAP Solution Manager, enterprise edition, this book first introduces the system monitoring concept and the SAP Solution Manager. It then discusses the all relevant aspects of system monitoring.
This guide is completely revised and updated for the enterprise edition of SAP Solution Manager, with new screenshots and additional content.

194 pp., 2. edition 2009, 69,95 Euro / US$ 84.95
ISBN 978-1-59229-308-7

>> www.sap-press.com

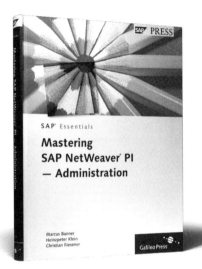

2nd edition, extended and updated
for SAP NetWeaver PI 7.1

Benefit from exclusive tips on
configuration, performance
optimization, and monitoring

Learn everything about SOA
integration and the Enterprise
Services Repository

Marcus Banner, Heinzpeter Klein, Christian Riesener

Mastering SAP NetWeaver PI - Administration

This practical SAP PRESS Essentials guide will guide you through all of the relevant
administration tasks involving SAP NetWeaver Process Integration, helping you to identify
and avoid the common pitfalls. The authors guide you through the configuration of
Enterprise Services Repository and the System Landscape Directory. Exclusive insights
help you to quickly learn the basics of configuring the System Landscape Directory and
Change Management Service. Plus, you get a highly detailed introduction to the XI
transport system. You'll learn about the crucial topics of authorizations and performance
optimization. This second edition has been updated and revised, and is up to date for
SAP NetWeaver PI 7.1. A new chapter covers the Enterprise Services Repository. With
this unique guide, you'll profit immediately from the authors' wealth of practical
experience, and you'll be fully prepared for the administration of SAP NetWeaver PI.

225 pp., 2. edition, 69,95 Euro / US$ 84.95
ISBN 978-1-59229-321-6

>> www.sap-press.com

Provides all functional details on the successor of CUA

Describes integration with SAP NetWeaver and SOA landscapes

Includes two detailed real-life scenarios

Loren Heilig

Understanding SAP NetWeaver Identity Management

Whether you're thinking about an identity management solution for your company, are currently implementing one, or are already working with SAP NetWeaver Identity Management, this book covers all important aspects for the selection, implementation, and operation of the solution. Take advantage of proven concepts and tips from the authors, and learn SAP NetWeaver IdM from A to Z.

300 pp., 2010, 69,95 Euro / US$ 69.95
ISBN 978-1-59229-338-4

>> www.sap-press.com

Interested in reading more?

Please visit our Web site for all
new book releases from SAP PRESS.

www.sap-press.com